PRACTICALLY PAGAN

An Alternative Guide to Magical Living

PRACTICALLY PAGAN

An Alternative
Guide to
Magical Living

Maria DeBlassie

MOON
BOOKS

Winchester, UK
Washington, USA

JOHN HUNT PUBLISHING

First published by Moon Books, 2021
Moon Books is an imprint of John Hunt Publishing Ltd., No. 3 East Street, Alresford
Hampshire SO24 9EE, UK
office@jhpbooks.net
www.johnhuntpublishing.com
www.moon-books.net

For distributor details and how to order please visit the 'Ordering' section on our website.

Design: Matthew Greenfield

UK: Printed and bound by CPI Group (UK) Ltd, Croydon, CR0 4YY
Printed in North America by CPI GPS partners

We operate a distinctive and ethical publishing philosophy in
all areas of our business, from our global network of authors to
production and worldwide distribution.

Contents

Introduction

Greetings, fellow magic seeker! If you've picked up this book, it means one of two things: You already believe in the reality of everyday mysticism, or you are curious about the possibility of a world more magical, more infinite than the one you currently inhabit. Maybe it's synchronicity that led you down this path— finding this book at the right place and the right time, perhaps after a fleeting thought that you want something more from your life but don't know how to get it or where to start. Maybe you've always known you were a little different, seeing the world as a fluid conversation between the seen and the unseen, the concrete and the ethereal, the worldly and the otherworldly. Or maybe you're just looking for a way to make the day-in, day-out mundanities feel like delicious delights you actually look forward to. Whatever the case, and however this book made its way into your hands, you've come to the right place.

I'll let you in on a little secret: This book is magic. All books are. So much so that they are picky about who picks them up and reads them. They only want people ready to hear their message, kindred spirits eager to soak up their specific brand of magic. If you've found this book, it's because it wants you to read it. So, when I call you a fellow magic-seeker, it is because this book only speaks to those in search of a little everyday magic. You may not even be sure what everyday magic is, exactly, but I promise you that by the end of this book, you'll learn not only what it looks like, but what it feels like deep in your bones, and how to conjure it in your own life.

Like all titles in the *Practically Pagan* series, this book is designed to show you a deeper way of living and experiencing the mystic, regardless of whether you identify as pagan or are simply curious about exploring various aspects of spirituality. It's a vast world out there, with many expressions of spirituality

1

unchained from traditional religion. The deeper you move into your own spiritual explorations, the more you will uncover a hidden metaphysical world and, more importantly, the magic inherent in our here and now. You'll also discover a wider community of wild hearts eager to transcend the limiting cultural beliefs that keep us from our true selves. I'll let you in on another secret: There are more of us out there than you think.

But before I go on, I should tell you that I practice a specific kind of magic intrinsically tied to my cultural background: *brujería*. This translates as *witchcraft* in English, but it's a little more than that. For starters, it is about reclaiming brown woman magic. I'm a mestiza, or mixed-race, woman from the American Southwest (New Mexico, to be exact), with Latinx, Indigenous, and European ancestry. One of the major reasons I identify as mestiza, like many others, is that I want to acknowledge that I am a product of colonization.

Mestizaje blood carries the history of the genocide of Native Americans, the oppression of non-white bodies, and the use of religion to control women's bodies and silence medicine men and *curanderas* (healers), among other practitioners of natural healing and spirituality. Ours is a history of cultural assimilation and white-washing. The history of the Spanish conquistadors is romanticized; Indigenous cultures are silenced and appropriated. The mestizaje acknowledges this history and reclaims the cultures colonization suppressed. To be mestiza is to grapple with the fact that you come from both the colonizers and the colonized, the conquistadors and the conquered, the natural witches, medicine men, curanderas—and the Catholic church.

So brujería is about reclaiming our power as brown, female bodies and acknowledging the ongoing violence and oppression that stems from our colonized past. It is about exposing the generational and ancestral trauma, results of those histories of violence, and, through that, reclaiming our capacity for joy. One present-day reality of our colonized past is that we've internalized institutionalized racism, sexism, and religious indoctrination, among other things—hard not to when they continue to be so culturally enforced. These toxic internalizations are so strong that we have to do a significant amount of work to heal ourselves and our communities, and move past these outdated narratives. We start that work by taking back our magic and reclaiming the once-derogatory term *bruja*. That was the catch-all phrase for anyone who did something the Spanish church did not understand and so feared. Curanderas, or local medicine women, who tended both spiritual and physical health; Native American medicine men who walked between worlds; and even local midwives, who seemingly had the power over life and death, were dubbed witches because they did the natural and metaphysical work the church couldn't understand and couldn't control. Calling ourselves brujas, then, is a way to celebrate those practices and our diverse background, even if we don't always have direct access to specific ancestral cultures or traditions. It is enough to know that we come from this mixed heritage, and, from there, forge our own path. I'm glossing over a lot of history and nuances here, but the gist of this mini history lesson is that when you have this kind of collective cultural memory written in your blood, you have to actively and consciously work through it. Otherwise, you'll find yourself perpetuating the trauma without even realizing it.

That's because your existence as a marginalized body is so regulated by mainstream culture that your life path options are seemingly limited. You are either invisible or suffering, silenced or oppressed. Mainstream culture allows for no other narrative. As a result, brujas have to learn how to create our own stories of joy, hope, and healing, and how to healthily live those stories out. Many have paved the way before me, and many will come after. This book is dedicated to the wild souls, those looking to free themselves from ancestral traumas and limited social norms designed to keep *othered* bodies down. That's what brujería is all about.

We create our own magic by daring to live a life that prioritizes self-care, pleasure, and wellness. We dare to imagine a world in which we too, can have Happily Ever Afters (HEAs as the readers of romance novels call it) and explore our infinite capacity for joy without guilt or shame, those products of old school religion that make us afraid of our bodies and passions. And we do it by creating space for difficult pasts, situations, and emotions, and by consciously working through them.

I know—this is heavy stuff for a book that's supposed to be about the sunshine and rainbows associated with the phrase "everyday magic." But here's the thing about magic: it's hard work! Part of finding your way to the sunshine and rainbows is weathering the proverbial storms. In short, this book is about our profound ability to conjure new narratives—narratives of hope and healing, particularly for othered bodies—as a form of everyday magic. You might not practice brujería. Again, this is a culturally specific term. I also only briefly outlined my expression of brujería and didn't even touch other forms of the practice in other Latinx cultures, including African, Caribbean, and Indigenous expressions of the craft. My own form of brujería is likewise different from other mestiza practitioners. But that's okay. You don't need to be Latinx or a woman in order to get wisdom from this book, or, if you are, you don't need to practice brujería in the exact same way I do. That's because this is not a book about brujería specifically. This is a book about everyday magic for any practitioner of any background, so the tips and advice I offer are not culturally specific.

Like I said earlier, this book chose you, so it has a lot of wisdom to offer you in your own journey into self, healing, and magic. I did want to let you know where I was coming from, however, because you'll be reading about things like ancestral trauma and internalized racism. Those have been some of the demons I've had to work through (and continue to) in my journey into everyday magic. You might not be working through those issues specifically—or just not know it yet—but the wisdom in this book can still help you heal your relationship with yourself, something we all must do in one way or another. Magical living is designed to help us work through those issues in safe, compassionate ways, so that we can allow ourselves to be more than our histories of oppression.

Likewise, magic is deeply personal and unique to each person, kind of like a signature. So, you'll see the imprint of brujería and the mestizaje all over my guide to everyday magic. I hope it inspires you to explore the areas in your life where you need healing, either from personal or ancestral issues. These wounds might be cultural, spiritual, gendered, social, political, archetypal, or any number of other charged areas. In all likelihood, they are intertwined with one another. I encourage you to see this book as an open invitation to begin exploring your own relationship to yourself and the mystic world.

A few more things you should know before we get into the how-to portion of this book. This is a *practical* guide to everyday magic, like the title suggests, which means it will be less *double double toil and trouble* and more...making soup. Hey, never underestimate the power of a good soup! It heals sickness, mends broken hearts, and soothes tired souls. That's the kind of magic I'm talking about. Let's look at this another way. There's often talk in the alternative spirituality communities about cleansing and protecting your home against negative energy. We charge crystals in moonlight to magnify healing energies and sage our houses (if culturally appropriate and not appropriated) to banish evil spirits and purify our space. But you know what else brings healing and cleansing energy into our homes? A solid scrub down. Seriously! Wash those floors. Dust those shelves. Fold that laundry. There's nothing like a little elbow grease to bring positive, healthy energy into your home and keep out unwanted bad vibes.

My personal relationship to magic is less about manipulating energies for desired outcomes and more about tuning into myself and my connection to the Universe. So instead of pushing for a specific outcome, I stop and ask why energy seems blocked in that direction. Maybe it means that is not the path for me, however much I think I want it (which is usually the case). Other times it might mean that I have to clear through something before I can move forward. Whatever the issues, I stop, think, and work on what the signs from the Universe are telling me. It's subtler magic, softer, asking me to listen rather than aggressively forcing something. I align myself with my inner voice, and the outer world responds with like energy.

Lastly, I'm a storyteller by nature, as much as I am a bruja. Like I said earlier, books and storytelling are some of the most potent spells out there, healing the soul and voicing truths that other forms of magic can't. There is magic in hearing a story and taking what medicine you need from it, magic in beginning to think of yourself as a story that you get to shape and create. I'll be telling you stories about my personal journey, so you can begin to think of your own journey as an unfolding narrative that you get to pen. You'll notice, too, that I draw on a variety of archetypes, from Greek mythology to native New Mexican lore—again, that's all part of what it means to be mestiza. We can't always access all the cultures that create our individual mix because of very real concerns about stirring up old traumas. You would be surprised by the kind of ghosts and demons that can get stirred up when someone reaches too far into the past, an issue that isn't often talked about when people try to reclaim specific cultural traditions. Sometimes we can't go back, plain and simple, however much we might want to. But we can call on the archetypes that speak to us. I'm also a professor by day, so you'll hear me talk about the magic of learning and unlearning as we begin to cultivate everyday magic. There is so much wisdom to be found in lessons learned, relearned, and unlearned. That's the good news. Everyday magic is just that—simple, accessible ways to conjure abundance, happiness, and health. The less exciting news? It's hard work (remember the elbow grease and intensive healing). Simple doesn't always mean easy, as any seasoned magical practitioner can tell you. Magic takes time, focused energy, commitment before you see results. I think of it as a garden. You have to tend it a little every day, each season demanding something new. If you don't, your plants die and your garden fades. But if you do care for it daily, then you are rewarded with an abundant harvest at the end of the season, before the cycle begins anew. Hard work, yes, but the joy that blossoms out of that labor is so incredibly worth it. And, perhaps unsurprisingly to the garden witches reading this book, joy can be found in the labor itself.

Now that you know what this book is about in general, it's time to break down how I organize things. Organization is, again, not something that feels too *hocus-pocus*, but necessary for magical living all the same. My first chapter explains what everyday magic is and recounts my journey back to finding my inner magic. I've then broken the subsequent chapters down into what I consider the five major parts of everyday magic: radical self-care, routine as ritual, pleasure magic, synchronicity, and exploring the energies of the un/expected.

In each chapter, you'll get definitions of each concept, real-life examples of how they play out, and, at the end, tips on how to develop these practices in your own life. These tips are broken into two sections: Routine as Ritual, or how to build this aspect of everyday magic into your day-to-day life; and Everyday Conjuring, or exercises and meditations for when you might need a little more *oomph* to find what best suits your needs.

There will also be some questions throughout the book for you to meditate on. These will help you begin to understand what you need to let go of, nourish, or make space for in your life. Half of conjuring everyday magic, as you'll see, is learning to tune into your inner voice and silence the outside world, which so often tells us to suppress our inner wild heart. The first four chapters are focused on how to invite mystic energy into your life and banish bad vibes; the final two are about being open to magic once you've embraced healing within and without. You'll see that these practices are interconnected, so that I often can't talk about one without the other. I end with a chapter on conjuring your own special magic. There, you'll learn what it means to develop an ongoing, fluid, mystic practice that is suited to your own energy and background.

The beauty of this book is that it offers a great starting point for discovering and cultivating your inner magic. Keep in mind what I said earlier, however. Magic is unique to each soul, so as you read each chapter, stay playful, explore, and learn what works best for you—and what doesn't. There is no right or wrong way to cultivate magic, so long as you are doing what makes you feel happy, healthy, and whole. In return, you cultivate a healing, nurturing relationship with the natural world and those around you. In fact, it's not a good idea to get too rigid about things or start seeing my guide as gospel. I mean, we've left mainstream religion for a reason, right? That reason, in part, is because individuation is an important part of self-empowerment, and, by extension, our natural magic. This is all to say that this book asks you to take what speaks to you and, from there, develop your own mystical practice. Like I said, there's a great, wide world of magical people out there, and not one of us experiences the mystical in the exact same way. Allow yourself to explore what everyday magic means to you.

And with that, it's time to get started. Welcome to the wonderful world of ordinary mysticism. And remember, as I say on my blog, true magic is in the everyday.

Chapter 1

What is Everyday Magic?

Over the years, I've written a lot about everyday magic, a term I use to describe the mysticism inherent in our day-to-day lives. In practice, this means cultivating joy and consciously letting go of negative patterns. It means listening to yourself and your needs. And it means having long conversations with the stars and giving yourself permission to dream deeply and with wild abandon, both at night, when you sleep, and during the day, when you can turn your daydreams into seeds for future happiness.

So where does the magic come in? When we think of magic, we think of wizards and witches with wands and cauldrons and grimoires. It's true, I call myself a bruja and, more specifically, a kitchen witch. It's also true that I have a cauldron—two, in fact. Only, I call them cast-iron pots. I even have a few spellbooks. They are the collection of family recipes written in a handmade book, the catch-all binders where I save my favorite recipes for roasted chicken or stew, and the well-used copies of my beloved collection of cookbooks. And that's just it: These simple, mundane things are actually full of magic. We just aren't always aware of it. Too often, we look for the sublime in things outside ourselves and neglect the beauty of what is right in front of us.

Think about it. How many times have you fantasized about throwing caution to the wind and moving to some far-off paradise in the hope that it will bring back your inner joy? How many times have you longed for an enchanted life—only to dismiss the little things that make your life wonderful? It's time to tune into these little delights and daily insights that are waiting at the bottom of a teacup or in the upturned face of a hollyhock. They are there, waiting to be noticed, waiting to share their magic, if only you open yourself to the Universe.

My Journey into Magic

I started my journey into everyday magic at a time when I had forgotten what it was like to wake up full of excitement to start the day. I was burned out. Graduate school can do that to you, as can juggling two or three part-time jobs at a time. Don't get me wrong, I was glad for those experiences and proud of earning my doctorate. But once I got stable work, I knew I didn't just have to *survive* anymore. I could live. I could have time for myself, unfettered by looming deadlines and exhaustion. For the first time in longer than I could remember, I had weekends. Real weekends, where I could do human-being things and sleep in. I knew where my next paycheck was coming from. That was the starting point for me. I'd achieved relative financial and professional stability (never underestimate the power of a steady paying job). Now I could focus on my internal life. Nourish my soul. Find my magic again.

I needed to remember who I was outside of external accomplishments and hard work—both of which I love if I'm completely honest, but a woman, especially a wild brown woman, can't survive on external achievements alone. I needed to return to a deeper way of living, one that didn't have me skating across the surface of life in a desperate attempt to please those who held my future in their hands. I could slow down and relish each moment as it unfolded. So, there I was, ready to dive head-first into my latest adventure of self-healing and self-discovery—a time I had been fantasizing about for years, so much so that it was the only thing that got me through my work sometimes.

There was only one problem. No sooner had I embraced my desire to reawaken my inner magic, than I'd been forced to confront one shocking secret: I was addicted to busy. I literally couldn't slow down. I was used to long days and quick meals.

Even shoulder pain from hunching over my desk felt like a normal part of my life, as did the inevitable griping over the proverbial water cooler at the office. I couldn't believe it. Me, the woman who, even at her most stressed-out and busy, still made time to clean her apartment and do the dishes after every meal. The woman who hated negative talk and gossiping. The woman who insisted on taking Sundays off and going on long walks through the city, because maintaining even a sliver of unstructured time just for myself was essential to my happiness—and my magic. Without even knowing it, I'd succumbed to superficial living by not caring for my body and feeding needless negativity, among other things.

Clearly, finding my way back to myself was going to be harder than I thought. I knew my magic was still there. It'd gotten me this far, after all. I wasn't so far down the road to mundane living that I couldn't acknowledge that my current success was due to the personal magic I'd cultivated all these years. It wasn't gone, just...dormant, tired, in need of tending. But I also knew that if I didn't start tending it more seriously, it would be gone. That's what long-term burnout and living inauthentically does. It depletes your magic.

This was when I first learned how hard it could be to live more consciously. I was no stranger to hard work, but I found that I had to get used to the idea of making space for personal wellness, seeing it as something that was just as valuable, if not more so, than my external accomplishments. In fact, all my external accomplishments, I now realize, came from a foundation of stability and self-care. Still, it took time to unlearn the guilt and the sense that I was being lazy I felt whenever I took time to rest or nurture myself—but more on that in the next chapter. It was even harder to let go of concrete or visible measures of growth. As a brown woman in academia, so much of my survival depended on proving my worth, over and over again, through concrete achievements. In fact, I'd realized that graduate school had been a series of check marks for each task completed; now, in my developing bruja lifestyle, I had no tangible way of understanding my progress. I only had how I felt, which made things difficult. I'd spent the greater part of the last few years second-guessing every feeling, every instinct I'd had because of imposter syndrome. The silencing I endured as a woman of color in the white space of higher education kept me from trusting my intuition.

So, I started blogging on the magic of everyday life. I needed a way to understand what made me happy and what didn't. I needed to find my voice outside of my professorial life. My writing has always been a source of healing and power for me, so it made sense that it would play an integral part in my journey back to my magic. I made a list of the things that blocked my energy—too many people, not enough quiet time, for example— and worked on eliminating them from my life. These things were actively making me feel tired, anxious, and heavy. Okay, so I knew what *wasn't* good for me. Then, I went about exploring what *was*.

Each day, once I committed to that first year of reclaiming my magic, I wrote a blog post, taking no more than twenty minutes to do so, reflecting on the things that made me happy. I filled my blog with recipes, pictures, and creative musings on simple pleasures and the difficulties of trying to carve out a more magical life for yourself in a world that would prefer you to be numb inside and therefore easier to manage. Even talking about the darker aspects of magic (what I call "everyday gothic") or living in a world that doesn't always value Divine Feminine energy was cathartic. Even posting imperfect work was delightful for me. Perfection had become an ugly cage that held me back from taking risks, both on the page and in my life. I reclaimed my power with each word I wrote. I also learned how to get more comfortable articulating my mestiza roots and exploring my culture on my own terms rather than performing what mainstream white culture or other mestiza voices wanted my relationship to my culture to look like.

I found others like me—people looking to reconnect with their natural mysticism and eschew mainstream culture. Mixed-raced people quietly exploring what that meant to them. Recovering academics rediscovering the joys of creating. It was a relief to know that I wasn't the only one struggling to return to my true self. These people made me feel brave. Gradually, one post at a time, one day at a time, I was able to return to myself. I started small, cultivating an awareness of what gave me energy and what took it. Gradually, I came to understand that each thing I had to let go of was intrinsically tied to three basic things I had to unlearn in order to create space for magic: Toxic Patriarchy, Performative Extroversion, and Mindless Busy.

Things I've Had to Unlearn

They seem so obvious now, but at the time, I was so entrenched in these social constructs that I couldn't seem to find my way outside them. Once I began to heal my relationship with myself, it was as if I had woken from a deep sleep. I could see these constricting ideologies like strands in a spider's web trying to pin me down.

Toxic Patriarchy

This is pretty much what it sounds like: any system or belief that mindlessly promotes toxic masculinity as the ultimate form of power. There is such a thing, after all, as healthy masculinity. Just look at the Emperor card in the tarot, or a good father. Each of them is a benevolent masculine force caring for those he loves. Toxic patriarchy, on the other hand, is all about control. Control over women's bodies, minds, and actions, not to mention anything that smacks of traditionally feminine traits, like one's emotional or internal lives. In fact, it has an unhealthy control over men's bodies, minds, and actions too—and it does

13

so to people who don't conform to the gender binary! This is an ideology, in short, that is harmful to people of all genders because it privileges extroversion, aggression, and force over more subtle forms of expression or empowerment.

I considered myself to be very in-tune with my feminine side, having grown up in a home that valued talking about our emotions, listening to our instincts, and finding wisdom in the dreams we'd had the night before. That said, I found that when I was in the wider world, I'd begun to shut down that part of myself in order to survive. As a minority in higher education—an institution that at its worst is designed to reinforce and privilege white, able-bodied, heteronormative cisgender patriarchy—I found myself continually apologizing for my presence there. Yes, I had allies, many of them who are still my good friends today. But that didn't change the fact that, as a twenty-something mestiza studying 18th Century British Literature, of all things, I was an anomaly in the Ivory Tower. In the worst cases, anything I did that was vaguely emotional was written off as female hysteria by some of my closest advisors. If I was too friendly, and I was labeled an over-sexed Latina. Things like close-knit family relationships were viewed as hindrances to furthering yourself in your profession, rather than an important part of your life. Unstructured or personal time was for lazy people. And forget taking care of yourself. Shoulder and neck pain from poring over books and back pain from sitting too long were like badges of honor for a hard-working scholar.

This was all the dark side of this experience, of course, and certainly plenty of good came of that time too. However, these toxic patriarchal messages were subtle and persistent, and, because I was so unconscious of them, I began to feel guilty when I took time for myself. I became numb to cope with the stress of feeling like I couldn't express my emotions without it devaluing my work. All in all, I look back on that time and realize I could have been an emotional, intuitive, self-care-focused woman, if only I had recognized the destructive ideologies at work and consciously countered them as I do now. But my impostor syndrome was so strong, as was the power of presumed incompetence, a term that means that anyone who isn't a white man in academia is assumed to be automatically incompetent. As a result, the more I felt called out for presumed incompetence or seemingly unprofessional behavior, the more I embodied those perceptions of myself.

Once I allowed myself to feel what I needed to feel, however, and acknowledged how divorced I'd become from the Divine Feminine within me, I began to heal. Better still, I found friends across gender expressions who experienced the same thing and took comfort in knowing that they, too, were committed to reclaiming their inner magic. Individually we learned that the destructive power of toxic patriarchy was in disconnecting us from ourselves and from forming healthy relationships with others. Together, we could resist toxic patriarchy and promote a healthier, more holistic form of education and relational living.

Performative Extroversion

The next thing I had to let go of was what I call performative extroversion, or always being loud, social, and surrounded by people. Let's face it, we live in a world that values extroversion — at work and at play. If you're not loudly proclaiming everything you do with all the people you do it with, then you're not a balanced human. This is all good and well if you are a natural extrovert. Yet that's a tough act to maintain for an introvert.

I'm a private person by nature, and I need my quiet time to feel fully recharged. If I don't have time to dream, take long, solitary walks, and putter about the house, I feel as if a deep part of me is missing. Don't get me wrong — I can enjoy being with people quite a bit. But I need time in between socializing for myself and my internal life. This is even more true because I have a pretty extroverted job as a teacher. I love every minute of it, but then I need time to go home, be quiet, and putter. I'm quite happy with this now, looking forward to the simplicity of my life, mostly because I see the direct correlation between my quiet alone time and my happiness. More quiet time equals greater happiness. But it wasn't always that way.

I used to get down on myself for being a natural introvert. It was nothing short of a minor miracle (more of that everyday magic) when I stumbled across an article in a hippy magazine. It gave me the term *introvert*, which described me so perfectly that I could have cried. I wasn't an anomaly. There were others out there like me.

Prior to that, however, I found myself in a cycle of what I could only call binge socializing. I'd go out a ton, then literally get sick and be forced to stay home and recuperate. The funny part was that even though I was sick, I relished that quiet time at home. I wasn't even aware of this cycle until I ran into a friend and mentioned that I was coming down with something. He observed that I always seemed to be ill. And he was right. It was a stunning revelation, and perhaps the first time I realized just how often I felt unwell. I had fallen out of balance, and getting sick was my body's way of making me stay home and tend my introverted soul. Clearly, I needed a lifestyle change.

I'm much better at tending my introverted needs now, through a lot of trial and error. It took me a long time to learn what types of socializing felt fun, and how often, and what was just plain draining. And while I still have times where I feel guilty for eschewing social obligations in favor of nurturing my solitude, I'm getting better at honoring my intrinsic makeup. The best part is, most of the people in my life are introverts too, so they understand when I'm looking forward to a weekend at home.

Mindless Busy

I've come to see *busy* as just another four-letter word. It's the sludge we hide behind when we don't want to (or feel like we can't) listen to our own needs. The world wants us to be constantly plugged in, constantly expending energy, constantly making noise. Moreover, we live in a society that values extroversion, overworking oneself, and excess over the softer virtues of introversion, meaningful productivity, and mindful consumption. It should come as no surprise that one of the last lessons I had to unlearn was mindless busy, that nausea-inducing feeling of moving so fast, doing so much, that you're dizzy with the effort. I lead a full life. Teaching, writing, and my personal life easily fill my days and evenings with much to enjoy. But this is different from mindless busy, which lacks intention or reason.

We all know what it is like to overwork or overcommit to things. I've certainly done my fair share of that in the past. It's that old impostor syndrome again, making me overcompensate for my insecurities. I've learned, however, to differentiate between a full, vibrant life and one in which I feel like I'm spinning my wheels and going nowhere. The first step towards that was learning how to say no—such a powerful word—to things, people, and situations that didn't enhance the overall quality of my life. I had to get used to drawing boundaries in my work life and aggressively creating space for my personal life (another example of healthy masculine energy, by the way).

I realized that mindless busy was a way of hiding out from life. If I was running from one thing to the next, I never had to really check in with myself and ask if I was happy, or what I might need to feel more fulfilled. If I always overcommitted, I never had to do the hard work of getting to know myself, something that felt truly scary once I realized how disconnected from myself, I'd become. Better to keep moving too fast than to stop, slow down, and confront the fact that I wasn't sure who I was anymore.

Then life slowed me down. I was just too worn out to keeping moving so fast. I took a summer off teaching. I traveled. I rested.

17

I got to know myself again outside of a rapidly ticking clock. It was delightful. I was now ready to discover what my life could be, now that I'd begun the process of unlearning toxic patriarchy, performative extroversion, and mindless busy. I found it in the Divine Feminine, Soulful Introversion, and Slow Living.

Things I Had to Relearn

Once I cleared the slate of things that were holding me back—or at least developed an awareness of how I unconsciously played into destructive mainstream culture—I needed to find my way back to the instincts I'd ignored for so long. Then came the slow, gentle study of things I had to relearn. Things that were inherent to my childhood, things I never used to have to think about twice. It should come as no surprise that these things were all in one way or another related to the Divine Feminine, or the strong healing goddess energy that runs in direct contrast to Toxic Patriarchy.

Divine Feminine

The Divine Feminine is the nurturing and creative energy within all of us, regardless of our gender. Think of her as Mother Nature or the archetypal goddesses that represent healthy sexuality and relationships. She's soft and lush and representative of all things ephemeral and intuitive. She works quietly, in the shadows, the passive Moon to the expressive Sun. While both energies are needed within us to thrive, the Moon asks us to explore the shadows, the unknown, the things we aren't comfortable with. The unspoken. The unseen. Basically, everything we are taught to fear—not because it is wrong, but because it represents a view of life that runs counter to what daylight tells us is important. Passivity doesn't mean powerlessness, as society teaches us. Rather, the Moon's less aggressive energy is about being open and receptive to the ebb and flow of life.

Tuning into the Divine Feminine taught me how to stop

trying to control a set life path or get rigid about manifesting a specific outcome. I learned that those things I thought I wanted often weren't what I needed or truly desired, when it came right down to it. That was why trying to get them felt like an uphill battle. Those paths weren't right for me, and deep down, I knew it. Sure, walking your true path requires a tremendous amount of energy and hard work, but once I'd learned how to be open to this gentle, guiding goddess energy, I realized that the kind of work it required didn't feel grueling. It just felt...right. Like I was doing what I was supposed to be doing.

Opening up to new possibilities of what my life could be, instead of what I thought it should be, allowed me to find my way back to magical living. A big part of this was drawing on the Divine Feminine to help me better listen to my intuition and instincts, which I'd been ignoring for quite some time. I'm not suggesting you throw common sense out the window, but sometimes we get so caught up in what mainstream culture says we should want and need that we forget to listen to our inner wisdom. Dating someone who seems "good on paper" is a good example of this; that list of external accomplishments and traits doesn't always speak to a solid foundation for a meaningful relationship. Once I started trusting my instincts, I saw a dramatic shift in how I viewed the world. Often, what seemed on the surface to be meaningful and important didn't hold up in the realm of the mystic. If I talked myself out of how I felt and did something that ran counter to my intuition, I paid a heavy price in energy. A job that I thought seemed great but didn't feel quite right ended up being a dead-end sinkhole, sucking up my time and energy with little to no financial compensation. I should have listened to what my instincts told me about this "opportunity," rather than let myself get talked into it.

Tuning into the unseen realm of vibes, energy, and flashes of insight gradually led me to an abundant outer life. And all because I chose to trust my goddess energy. The world opened up to me because I opened up to the world, via my vital expressions of self-care and self-love. The beauty of this relational energy: It helps us relearn how to have healthy, pleasurable relationships with ourselves, others, and the Universe.

Soulful Introversion

The Divine Feminine is what made it possible for me to recognize I was an introvert and absolutely needed space for my solitude in order to thrive. Once I discovered a direct correlation between over-socializing and poor mental and physical health, I could begin to be more sensitive to my needs. I learned to check in with myself. Did I get excited at the prospect of going to certain events, or did the idea of them make me anxious? How did I feel around certain people, replenished or depleted? What did I look forward to during that day, and what did I start to dread? These are the questions I asked myself so I could relearn what types of community and socialization actually nourished me and what didn't. I allowed myself to feel what I needed to feel and, slowly but surely, got used to giving myself permission to enjoy quiet time.

It seems funny now, but there was a time when I literally thought something was wrong with me for being an introvert. Well-meaning people in my life told me I needed to get out more or find more friends. Time at home, to them, meant I was doing nothing—dying of boredom and super lonely. That couldn't have been further from the truth. I had plenty of friends and social outlets (thankfully, many of them populated by fellow introverts). And when I was home, I enjoyed every quiet, blissful minute of it. In fact, the only times I've felt incredibly lonely was when I went out too much, was around too many people, or was around people who didn't understand the power of creating space to converse with the stars and watch butterflies dancing in the breeze. That was because I would lose my connection to myself. I suppressed my magic to be more appealing to the non-magical.

Honoring my introverted nature allowed me to get to know myself again. I stopped putting myself down for not being an extrovert, because I saw that my well-being was more important than any temporary relief that came from conforming to the status quo. Then a funny thing happened. The more I gave myself the home time I craved and the quiet I so desperately needed, the happier I became. My creativity flowed. My energy opened up for life and exciting new adventures. New work opportunities unfolded. My personal life developed naturally as I let myself be drawn to things that inspired me.

My intuition, too, grew even stronger as I dove into a more soulful way of engaging with the world. Instead of second-guessing my instincts and feelings, I listened to them—and they were never wrong. I only ever got into trouble when I ignored the vibes I was picking up. I'd had more than a few uncanny experiences that lead me to fully embraced my introverted nature.

For example, I had been hemming and hawing about attending a social event an acquaintance desperately wanted me to attend. It seemed like it should be fun—many people I liked would be there, and I always loved a lively intellectual conversation, which this event promised. The day of the event, though, I grew more and more anxious the closer I got to the time. My stomach was in knots and my shoulders ached from tension. There was no way I could go to the party feeling like that, so I canceled my plans. Within half an hour I had begun to feel better, and ended up having quite a lovely evening at home cooking, listening to jazz records, and reading. I chalked the whole thing up to being an introvert and even inwardly rolled my eyes at my inability to attend even one harmless gathering now and then.

The next time I saw my friend, however, I learned that the party had been nothing short of traumatizing. I won't go into the details (lest I inadvertently conjure bad-vibe energy by talking for too long about it), but suffice it to say the evening had been full of petty dramas and full-on meltdowns, mindless chatter and surface relationality. In short, it had been an empty, soulless gathering. Not my idea of a good time. And while they were dealing with the kind of superficial toxicity that I'd come to dread from many a party, I had spent a lovely, restorative evening enjoying high-vibration activities.

After that incident, I no longer forced myself to go out or hang with certain people if I wasn't feeling it. I wanted only positive, healthy relationships in my life, and if that meant I had fewer close friendships, then that was fine by me. I was too happy, too full of life when I honored my introverted needs, to compromise it with mindless socialization.

Slow Living

I'm still learning this one. Before, it was because I was so afraid to say no. Now? I get so excited about life that I want to say yes to everything! For the first time in my life, I'm learning what it means to slow down, even when it means saying no to what might be exciting projects. I pause. I consider it. I ask myself if I really have the time and energy to commit to another project and do right by it. More often than not, I'm reminded that my life is full, and the things I choose to give my time and attention to flourish because I deliberately choose not to overextend myself.

I'd also realized that I'd become addicted to mindless busy, as I mentioned earlier. It was safe. A space that, while lacking in magic, was comfortable, familiar. Slowing down forced me to look at why I was moving too fast. My reasons were rooted in fear and anxiety. What if I made space for other non-tangible parts of my life and...nothing came of it? What if I stopped trying to juggle so much and discovered that my life was empty?

I had to try. Mindless busy certainly wasn't making me happy. And the truth is, things did feel empty at first, as I got used to being more deliberate about what I let into my life. I had to clear out a lot before I could welcome in the good. But then the good came. When it did, it was shocking to see how fast I'd been moving and how much of what I did had been, well, kind of pointless. So much of what I'd filled my life up with before had been useless stuff done out of anxiety and nervous energy. I became calmer, happier.

I realized my happiness came from the fact that I'd created space for my magic to blossom. I'd decluttered my life—letting go of meaningless commitments, unhealthy relationships, and, yes, even literally cleaning out my home—so much so that I could finally see what I did have in my life. The commitments, people, and things I kept were what I truly valued. Everything else had been unnecessary and under nourishing. I found my magic in the freedom I'd carved out for myself. My writing opened up to me, as did the realm of the imagination. My body began to heal itself as I now had time to properly care for it. My soul began to delight in the littlest of pleasures because it was no longer numbed out from moving too fast.

Other people noticed this change too. Often, they would comment on how cheerful I always seemed, and how healthy. My outer world had become a reflection of my inner world—thanks to the hard work I put into reclaiming my magic. It was hard going at first, but then, I couldn't say when or how, the changes became visible to anyone and everyone I'd crossed paths with.

Magic is like that. It waits, and it watches to see if you are doing the work. And then, when the time is right—no sooner and no later—what you wished for begins to unfold, assuming your wish was meant for you. If not? You get something more beautiful, more wondrous than you ever could have imagined.

You might be wondering now what all this learning and unlearning has to do with magic. It's simple, really. By unlearning toxic things we've been taught about our lives, our selves, and our relationships, we create room for healthy, healing energy to flow into our lives. When we relearn the power of joy, listen to our inner voice, and cultivate meaningful relationships, we welcome abundance into our day-to-day. That's where the magic comes from.

Finding Our Way Back to Magic

When we think of daily life, we tend to focus on the less alluring parts of it: getting stuck in traffic, folding clothes, grocery shopping. We get tired, and we get crabby. We just want to relax. But what if the traffic jam is life's way of reminding you to slow down? That extra time allows you to check in with yourself. Breathe. Maybe even listen to a few songs on the radio as your mind wanders freely. You'd be surprised by the insights that hit when you give yourself that time. Same goes for laundry. Nothing says self-care more than the mundane meditation inherent in making your way through a basket full of clean clothes. And the trip to the grocery store? Bliss. Seriously! It's gathering supplies for spells and medicine and nourishment for the week, a study in intentional living.

That's everyday magic. Looking for the beauty in the little things too often overlooked in our rush to get from one place to the next. Let's face it: Most of us lead lives that are far busier than we'd like them to be. All this hustle and bustle makes it too easy to overlook the simple pleasures that revive our senses and nourish our soul. Forget living fast—it's time to break up with that addiction and turn our energy towards a more grounded, joyful way of living.

Then, when we stay conscious and tuned into the daily beauty of our lives, the mystic world opens up to us. We become attuned to the subtle forces that only make themselves known to us when we take the time to listen, breathe, and connect with the Universe. Think about it. We've all experienced uncanny or synchronous things in our lives that just can't be explained by conventional logic. We know what it's like to feel off, or to step into a place with bad vibes. Likewise, we instinctually feel happiness in a good home or while around kindred spirits. We've all had those random strokes of luck or meaningful coincidences that lighten our day, or strange epiphanies that guide us back to where we are meant to be. And yet, we rarely think of these things as *magical*. But they are.

You don't have to be a character in a fantasy novel, or even committed to an elaborate occult practice, to feel the magic in and around you. All you have to do is listen. Look. Wait. And be prepared to find the divine in everything, including yourself. You are, after all, magical, whether you realize it or not. We all are. It's just that most of us have forgotten how to conjure it or conjure in a way that isn't completely conscious.

We cast spells constantly. Every hope, every wish, every dream is a spell cast out into the Universe until it is ready to come to fruition. Every time we say goodbye to something toxic and hello to something life-affirming, we conjure happiness. When we've given too much, or are doing something that goes against the grain of who we are, we lose our magic—our mojo, as the expression goes. Only by being true to our nature can we conjure—and keep—our magic.

You might be wondering what magic looks like. This can be a hard question to answer if you are used to tuning it out. You'll find it in the tingling in your spine when something is not quite right, or the butterflies in your stomach when you know an adventure is just around the corner, or even in waking up ready to greet the day. It's in the flashes of synchronicity, and lightning that illuminates things that go bump in the night, and your hidden fears that only a dark and stormy night can make you face. It's in watching a ladybug crawl along the leaves of an artichoke plant or losing track of time blowing bubbles with little ones. It's making a wish on a burning candle and sending it out to the Universe. Most of all, it's in learning the story of yourself, the magical being always unfolding, always growing, like an eternally sprouting seed.

So how do you tap into this kind of magic? Take a deep breath.

Close your eyes. Let your energy settle. And when you open your eyes again, tune into the little details you often overlook. The richness of your coffee. The sweet hint of cedar perfuming the early morning air. The soft fuzz of your sweater kissing the inside of your elbows. Let go of the noisy nonsense that clutters up your day and create space for the delightful. That's when the magic happens.

But fair warning: magic doesn't come easily.

Magic is a Hard, Gritty Thing

Like I said earlier, when I truly committed to a magical life, I was stunned by how hard it was to learn how to surrender to the Divine Feminine energy. The mysticism inherent in our daily lives, the sacred simple pleasures that heal the soul, and the radical self-care that keeps us vital are hedonistic delights that enrich our sense of self and connection to the Universe.

Sounds lovely, doesn't it? And it is. But magic is also a hard, gritty thing. It takes its own time and works in its own way. When you ask the Universe for something, it waits and watches and looks to see if you are, in fact, doing your part to make that desire come to fruition. It asks for blood and sweat, time and tears, focus and energy. So, when you ask for your heart's desire, the Universe first considers whether it is a wise wish or an unhealthy infatuation. In time, if it's the right thing for you, then the wish whispered on a dandelion head will make its way back to you. Just as soon as it pleases and no sooner. Let's face it. If magic were easy, more people would be doing it.

The hardest part about magic is that you have to let go of any notion that you can control all the variables in your life. Surrender. Listen to the Universe and your heart of hearts. They will tell you where you need to go—and it's often not where you think you should be headed. Magic is tricky that way, revealing its wisdom only when you're committed not to a specific outcome but to the art of learning about yourself and the cosmic world around you.

It works kind of like this: When you ask for light, you might expect fireworks to go off in the night sky immediately. In reality, after hard labor, constant focus, and everyday conjuring, you get a small spark which you then nourish into a healthy fire to warm your home. You get the light you asked for, but in order not to take that conjuring for granted, you have to continue to work to keep it alive.

Magic is a lot like self-care in that way. When we talk about taking care of ourselves, it's often about pampering—lighting scented candles, sinking into bubble baths, taking afternoon naps. Rarely do we talk about the hard work that goes into actual self-care, like waking up before sunrise to exercise because that's the only time you know you can do it, or swearing off processed sugar because you know that as good as it might taste, it's not good for you. Self-care is letting go of toxic situations and people, regardless of what outsiders might think of your actions, so that you can feel at peace. It asks you to prioritize yourself without guilt in a world that sees that as a selfish act. In short, self-care requires some serious adulting.

As does magic. You walk the fine line between infinite belief and hard labor. As the common saying with writing goes, inspiration will never find you unless you're working. Neither does magic. It doesn't give anything away for free or shower you with unearned gifts. There's always a price. The best magic, your own conjured magic, tastes all the better because it was birthed from your own sweat, and, okay, sometimes tears.

So, you plant your soul seeds—those kernels of wisdom and insights that help us grow, flourish, and tend our inner landscape—and you tend them without rigid expectations. Then one day, those seeds will sprout, blossom, and ripen into delicious fruit, if that is what is meant to happen. Those that weren't meant to be find their purpose in feeding the worms in your compost bin. But the fruit you do harvest is nothing short of divinity. It tastes of your backyard, kissed by your sunlight. Fed by your dirt and watered by your sweat. It is summer in your mouth, the promise of eternal sweetness.

You get the idea. Magic is a hard, gritty, beautiful thing.

Conjuring Everyday Magic

Congratulations! You've made it this far, reading about unlearning toxic beliefs, relearning your profound capacity for joy, and the incredible work that goes into choosing a magical path. Glad to know I haven't scared you off.

Now we're ready to get conjuring. I'll be honest and tell you that it's going to feel a little weird at first. You'll wonder if you're doing what you need to. If you're doing something wrong. If you're doing something right. If you're doing anything at all. Don't worry. Those are all normal feelings. Just keep practicing (more on that below). Your senses will become more honed, and the magic will sneak up on you. One day, you'll feel the bliss hit and know that all your hard work has paid off.

But don't forget to keep at it. After all, once you have the magic, you can easily lose it. We too often take our inherent witchiness for granted. We get cocky. We forget how unhappy we were when we succumbed to more mundane—but socially acceptable—forms of being. We think we will always have access to this well of healing mysticism. But it can, and will, dry up if we go back to living badly, especially when we know better. Despite what we're taught in the self-help community, wellness and mystic joy aren't something you gain and then just have. You have to continue to work on it daily, like exercise or diet. The Universe needs to know you are working for happiness, not waiting for miracles to fall in your lap. You have the power to create the life you want, and, as you do so, you just might stumble across a miracle here or there. So yeah, this book is about learning how to conjure magic—and keep it. And when you struggle at the start of your journey, remember that we all have a little witchiness in us. We just need to tend it to see it blossom.

Questions to ask yourself:

What keeps me from slowing down?
What do I need to let go of?
Where is magic missing in my life?

Routine as Ritual: Preliminary Explorations of Everyday Magic

Wake Up Earlier.
I know, not everyone is a morning person like me, but it is so worth waking up a little earlier. I love the early morning quiet before the rest of the world is up. It's a perfect time to do yoga, drink a cup of coffee, and mull over the previous night's dreams. Sometimes, if I'm up early enough, I even get to write a little. This morning hush is what I like to call the *Realm of Possibility*, where anything can happen, where you create space for yourself and your needs, while setting your intention for the day. If I don't get that time, I find the rest of the day is harried, stressful, and much too hectic. A quiet early morning does much to help us tune into the magic of the day before we get swept away by our workload. Of course, if this doesn't work for you, consider your natural rhythms and find a schedule that works for you — just make sure to leave time first thing when you wake up for yourself.

Do One Thing Each Day That Makes You Happy.
Make this one thing that makes you happy in your day something that isn't related to work, exercise, or basic chores. For me, it's listening to audiobooks at work. I like to be carried away by a story while I'm doing mundane tasks or to dip into my latest

read during my lunch break walk. It revives and refreshes me like nothing else. This is akin to inviting happiness into your life and giving yourself permission to find joy in the little things. Once you choose your simple pleasure of choice, see how it affects you. Does it sweep away stress? Make you feel lighter? If the answer to those questions is yes, then keep doing it.

Maintain Awareness of Your Energy Throughout the Day.
We tend to go on autopilot, so in the early stages of recovering your magic, develop your awareness of the things you do mindlessly. This could be anything from working and running errands, to eating, or scrolling through your various social media newsfeeds. Then pause and think. Are they contributing to your overall sense of wellness? Or are they just things you do because you've always done them? If you stopped doing them, what would you do instead? For example, I found myself running too many errands each week after work, which left me feeling exhausted once I got home. I also found that I was always trying to squeeze just one more thing in at work, so much so that I seldom had time for myself to just breathe or think about the value of the additional work I was taking on. I cut back on unnecessary errands, limiting myself to two or three a week, and I began to give myself 24 hours to think about it before I committed to another project. The results? I committed to a lot less. I got home earlier and less tired, excited to cook and relax instead of collapse on the couch in a tired heap. Every time I felt myself losing my awareness, I tuned into why that was happening. It usually meant I was moving too fast—a great way to disconnect yourself from your magic—and I had to make a conscious effort to slow down and consider why I was spinning my wheels.

Everyday Conjurings: Awakening the Magic Within

Take a Chore You Dread and Meditate on Its Healing Power.
I know it sounds corny, but it works. Take something you hate doing—like paying bills or cleaning the shower—and reframe it in terms of the life you are creating: paying off debt, having a shower worthy of a sea goddess...okay, that may be going overboard, but you get the idea. We take ourselves and our hard work for granted, as we do all the seemingly less-than-glamorous aspects of our lives. It's easy to feel magical when we're reading witchy books and shuffling our tarot decks. But magic is also in the day-in, day-out things that we do to manifest the life we want. So, the next time you do laundry, think about how healing it is to have a pile of freshly cleaned clothes, that lovely armor that helps you navigate the world. Or appreciate taking your pets to the vet because they are your familiars and caring for them is an act of love.

Spend Five Minutes Every Day Creating Space for Magic.
It's just five minutes. It can be while you're stuck at a red light on your drive home from work, or in those last few minutes your dinner cooks in the oven. It can even be while you wash off the day in the shower. The more mundane the circumstances, the better. Use this time to just be open, aware of the magic flowing in and around you. Don't think too hard about anything or try to force a specific outcome. Just feel the ephemeral energy surrounding you, paying special attention to where it might seem stuck—imagine untangling those parts so they are free-flowing once again. This little exercise will help you loosen up and get playful, releasing any blockages and stagnant energy, so that you can begin to feel the magic flow in all aspects of your life.

Think About One Thing That Made Your Day Wondrous.
This is a great exercise to close out the day. Too often we go to bed overly tired, which is when negativity can set in. We can start thinking ugly, heavy thoughts about our lives, simply because we are tired. Don't feed the beast. Don't feed the dark energy that gets constellated when you indulge petty thoughts or negative self-talk. Instead, clear your mind and consider one thing that surprised, inspired, or moved you in the day. It can be something as mundane as starting a book you've been dying to read, or as uncanny as dreaming about something the night before and then having the same thing happen that day (trust me, it's a thing that has happened to me on more than one occasion). This way, you end your day and begin your dreaming time attuned to the magical. Better yet, you begin the following day predisposed to tune into your synchronous messages and magical happenings.

Chapter 2

Radical Self-Care & The Goddess Within

It sounds simple. *Take care of yourself.* Yet there are so many demands that come our way in the adventure that is life. We push ourselves hard. We doubt ourselves. We try out this and that. But so often, in the flurry of our daily routine, we forsake our self-care and, by extension, our sense of self. When we lose that connection, we lose our magic.

After all, tending ourselves in all aspects is like a continuous healing ritual. Building our energy, conjuring happiness, banishing stress and negativity. We can't grow and thrive without tending ourselves like we would the plants in our garden or our loved ones. Even knowing this, however, it can be easy to forget the importance of the self. This is partially because we are taught that selflessness is a virtue and that over-extending ourselves is proof of our commitment to our job, families, or passions. Nothing could be further from the truth. The reality is that healthy boundaries make for a happy life. Drawing limits on the things that demand more and more from you without reciprocating that energy is an integral part of creating space for magic. We aren't meant to keep giving. Like nature's cycles, we have prolific periods and fallow periods, high output times and restorative seasons. Self-care is about tuning into those natural rhythms and honoring that our energy isn't infinite.

The scary thing is that the further we get away from ourselves and our natural cycles, the harder it can be to get back on track, because we become so comfortable with the numbing routine. It's seductive in its own way. We live in a culture that values the collective group-think, overwork, and busyness, so much so that our sense of worth is based on how much we do and, in some shocking cases, how beat up our body and souls are. If you don't have battle scars from overwork, are you really giving it your all? That's the kind of toxic ideology that conjures negative energy and promotes stagnation.

I remember at one point in the early years of being a graduate student, I was talking with some of my peers. What had started as a conversation about our teaching and scholarly work slowly devolved into a laundry list of aches and pains that we'd incurred from too many hours at the desk. For one person who had lower back pain, someone else was sure to elaborate on the specifics of their brutal shoulder injury and another emphasized the almost-debilitating quality of their chronic headaches. It was as if we were trying to out-do one another's bodily pain and emotional fatigue to prove that we were the most dedicated to our crafts. I left that impromptu discussion feeling even more exhausted than usual and more than a little burdened by the weight of our collective burnout.

Where had our mind-body-spirit connection gone? When had we begun to celebrate imbalance? Then I realized that we were all caught in a performative trap. We worked in a profession that valued intellect over body and spirit, so it only made sense to us fledgling scholars to prove our commitment to our work by honing our intellect at the expense of our body and spirit. We had grown afraid of the things that made us feel vulnerable: our bodies, our emotions, all those intangible things that could get hurt under the searing gaze of the logic and reason so highly valued in higher education.

Fortunately, a lot of that is changing (although not fast enough, in my perspective). I think enough educators went through what we did and know that they don't want to pass on the trauma of not being allowed to be a whole human as well as an intellectual. Of course, there are still plenty of old school academics out there—I've just learned to distance myself from the toxic aspects of the Ivory Tower. That's how self-care magic works. We learn to take better care of ourselves so that in turn we take better care of the people in our lives, from those we work with to those we love. We break the toxic cycle of ill health and conjure healing energy through our commitment to balance and well-being.

After that fateful hallway conversation, I began to think more critically about my self-care habits (or lack thereof). I began to have more meaningful conversations about health and wellness with peers, friends, and family. One of the striking revelations I came to was from conversations with women of color in higher education. We discovered that few, if any, of us had healthy examples of successful people of color in our chosen fields. Sure, there were plenty of accomplished people. Plenty of hardworking and respected people. But most of them seemed overworked, stressed, and unhappy in their personal lives—if they were even able to carve out space for one. We unconsciously internalized that model of "success", one that values concrete, external accomplishments over a more holistic sense of balanced living. Slowly, we began to explore what it meant to live a balanced life. My friends and I made an effort to get together off campus and talk about things outside of our work. I started carving out more time for cooking, meditating, yoga, and rest. I gave myself breaks, went to art shows, took naps, and read trashy books. And, over time, I began to heal.

The funny thing? My life is just as full now as it was then (notice I avoided the term busy), but I am so much healthier. The reality I had to confront all those years ago is that I worked myself to the bone because I felt guilty about taking care of myself. Yet if I had committed to a regular self-care practice sooner, I would have gotten just as much done, but more joyfully, without pain, and in less time. The new self-care plan that came out of these life lessons was about being actively aware of how I can get sucked into overwork to assuage impostor syndrome or other self-doubts, and consciously resisting the traps that made me feel bad about taking care of myself. All those years ago, I had given up more than just feeling good about my body and soul when I overworked. I had given up my connection to the Goddess, that divinely radical energy that was my power source. She isn't any one archetype, she is many, and she comes to us when we are most in need of healing our relationship to our feminine energy, regardless of our gender. I had been actively working against myself. In short, I had disempowered myself when I stopped valuing my happiness and overall wellness.

Enter the Goddess. She is there to remind us that we are here to live radically. Joyfully. Without shame or censor. Which is why I've come to see my self-care practice as a radical act and a form of social justice. Radical self-care is the art of learning yourself, your needs, and what you need to do in order to nourish your mind, body, and soul. These needs often run counter to what mainstream culture tells us we should need, want, or have, which is what makes caring for yourself so—you guessed it— radical. There's an old witchy adage that I love: *As within, so without.* While this saying speaks to many things about life, in terms of self-care, it means that when we don't take time to tend our souls, we cannot experience genuine fulfillment in the outer world. When we tend our inner life and body, our outer world begins to reflect the positive changes we've been working on in ourselves. For example, when we let go of toxic people, we create space for healthy relationships, or when we give up junk food, we understand what it means to take pleasure in a healthy body.

In essence, radical self-care is about acknowledging the divinity of our mind, body, and spirit and caring for them accordingly. Lest this start sounding too religiously dogmatic or rigid, along the lines of the saying "my body is a temple," it's good to remember that the Greek Dionysus and the Roman Bacchus were also divine beings. This is all to say that while I am all for healthy, balanced living, I am against seeing our bodies as inherently impure or in need of constant cleansing, like many people who volley around the temple metaphor tend to do.

Radical self-care is about, in part, enjoying the hedonism those partying gods can help conjure. So, enjoy that glass of wine as much as you do your kale salad. Think about it: Radical. Self. Care. Not telling yourself to do more. Not telling yourself to be more. Not checking off arbitrary boxes of self-fulfillment. Not imposing unrealistic ideals on yourself. Just taking better care of yourself. This is more challenging than it seems because it requires you to truly listen to yourself, your body, your mind, your soul. It's no small task in a world that can demand too much of us and make us forget what genuine self-care looks like. To help chart my self-care progress, I came up with two guiding questions:

What will bring me joy?
What is sustainable?

First, if something doesn't contribute to my overall happiness and health, I let it go. It's as simple—and as hard—as that. We live in a world that tells us more is better, so I must continually relearn the joys of less. I must also be honest with myself about what brings me joy (hint: it's often not what society says will make me happy). Second, I've had to think about the long-term substantiality of any new self-care routine I want to incorporate into my life. Working out an hour a day at the gym is not realistic for me, with my teaching and writing schedule, and neither is cooking an elaborate meal from scratch every night. But walking five days a week around my neighborhood is doable, as is whipping up a simple soup or salad to enjoy in the evening. If my goal starts making me feel spread thin, I ditch it.

Self-care is also about not being too hard on yourself when you overindulge or skip exercise one too many times. Negative self-talk doesn't help anything. Looking for the root of the problem does. I always ask myself why I fell out of my self-care routine. It's usually because of overwork or stress—things in life we can't always control. We can, however, control our responses to them and work on committing to less when possible. Life is full of signs, and when I find myself unable to heal or destress, I think of those as signals that I'm out of balance. Even better, I remind myself that I have the power to restore that balance.

In the end, isn't balance and the healthy connection between mind, body, and soul what magic is all about? The irony of committing to self-care is that you rarely have tangible evidence of your growth, only the fullness in your chest that tells you that you're living well. It is so deeply personal that only your bones and heart whispering their contentment tell me that you am truly listening to your needs. That's the Goddess speaking.

When we tap into this Goddess energy by unifying our bodies, minds, and spirits, we return to our magic. We have more time to take in the wider world around us. We create space to converse with the stars, ask the moon questions, and share our deepest wishes with the Universe—and hear them respond in turn. When we forget to nourish everyday magic through self-care, we forget to live. It can sometimes feel like a long road back to a well-rounded self. But you can't get there until you first unlearned the toxic beliefs that disconnect you from the Divine Feminine. In order to heal, you must become your very own Persephone, at home in the Underworld and the world above, fluent in the language of the psyche and grounded in the routine of daily life. You must walk through Hell, know your demons and remember that angels walk among us.

Self-Care Principles I've Had to Unlearn

Much of what I've had to unlearn about self-care deals with its more performative aspects—those Instagrammable workout goals, meal plans, and other easily calculated formulas for wellness. Those are the trappings of the commercialization of self-care, not self-care itself. At the end of the day, self-care is messy. Self-care is hard work. Self-care isn't about how you look or how the world sees you, it's about how you feel inside. It's a perpetual healing spell you work on every minute of your waking hours—and every moment of your dreaming hours.

Self-care is Selfish.

Too often, self-care is considered another word for selfishness. If you're prioritizing yourself, it's assumed, you aren't doing your best to help others. This is an especially insidious idea when you're a minority, as too often you're asked to work harder, taking on emotional labor and social justice work without adequate compensation. We value the collective over the individual in many ways, so when a person decides to remove themselves from the collective, even for a little while, it is considered a betrayal. After all, why would a person need to take time for themselves if the community gives them everything they need? The idea that a person might have different or singular needs, and time alone to tend themselves, is terrifying because it calls into question the sanctity of the communal.

It is this desire for differentiation that gives self-care such a negative connotation. People fear difference, otherness, so when you separate from the herd to tend to your own needs, you make others uncomfortable. Hence self-care being considered "selfish" instead of "healthy." This is different, by the way, from healthy relationality and interconnectedness, which nourishes both communities and individuals.

So be selfish. Or, better yet, redefine selfishness as giving yourself permission to rest and rejuvenate. It's okay to take time for yourself! In fact, it's a necessary ingredient to magical living. And if it takes you time to build up the courage to disconnect from the collective to practice selfishness, then go ahead and acknowledge that a healthy you is better for your community too.

Self-love is a Form of Vanity.
My commitment to radical self-care inadvertently had a polarizing effect on people. On the one hand, fellow self-care practitioners and friends on their own healing journeys completely understood my drive to heal myself. On the other, people got caught up in the more physical aspects of self-care—fitness, diet, grooming. Without realizing it, my body had become a battleground. So much emphasis was placed on my physical appearance that I began to feel self-conscious about wanting to take better care of myself, lest I be accused of being vain.

But what's wrong with wanting to feel pretty? What's so bad about wanting to feel good about yourself? What's the matter with taking pride in your appearance? Three questions, one answer: Absolutely nothing. I have to remind myself of this every time I'm made to feel embarrassed about my desire to feel and look good. If I wear a pretty dress or eat a balanced diet, it's suggested that I'm doing it for the Male Gaze, or because I'm prioritizing prettiness over smarts. Much of this stems from our collective fear of the empowered female body and from the natural sensuality that emerges when you are taking care of yourself.

These limiting voices—the ones that critiqued every step along my healing process—inadvertently revealed that they couldn't possibly believe that a woman (of color) can be a multidimensional human being, one who likes beautiful dresses as much as she likes big books. That she can take supreme joy in caring for herself, and that it *is* for herself, not for the patriarchy. My healing journey became, in part, about shamelessly embracing my multifaceted nature. I am allowed to want to feel sexy. I am allowed to enjoy clothes that make me feel beautiful. I am allowed to enjoy the transformation of my healing body, both inside and out.

Self-care is a Universal, Set Process.
The one thing that stays consistent in my self-care practice is that it changes a little every year as my own needs change and I become more sensitive to myself. One summer, I went regularly to a local gym and, between that, yoga, and dance, I spent the summer exercising a good two to three hours a day. This was in part because I was trying to figure out what types of physical exercise worked best for me and my body, and in part because I was having fun exploring new communities. I'd just finished my first book manuscript and was enjoying a fallow, restorative period. Less time writing meant more time to explore my self-care needs. All good and well, except that when fall started and I was back to teaching, all that went out the window. I didn't have extra energy to drive to the gym or stay up late on a Friday night to make it to that week's big Latin dance event. And forget yoga studio practice—I was lucky if I got in a good forward bend before I went to bed.

The reality of my predicament came crashing down. Those activities were great during the summer when I had a flexible schedule and more extroverted energy at my disposal, but they weren't sustainable in the long term. Even the next summer, I found myself with no desire to go back to that rigorous schedule. I was learning that a huge part of my overall well-being was in having unstructured time. Running from one thing to the next made it so that I could never settle down or decompress after a long workday. I'd also begun writing more steadily again. I enjoyed the freedom of having time for my words without committing to more social activities that often drained rather than replenished me when I was teaching. So, there I was, once again retooling my self-care routine.

I scaled back on everything: work, scheduled workouts, regular social events. I made time for quiet. I acknowledged that I was not a limitless fountain of energy and that, between teaching and writing and my personal life, I was extroverted enough. I was allowed to have my solitary time. The rest of my life was full to brimming with joyful human interaction, when I looked at it. I didn't want more—just time to let my imagination wander where it would and my soul to fill up on garden herbs and tortilla making. My exercise took the form of gardening and house cleaning, long walks and yoga on my old-as-sin mat rolled out in a corner of my home. Cooking and eating became a ritual in living a slow, delicious life. I let myself have what my body, mind, and spirit had been begging me to give them all along: slowness, softness, quiet. I healed.

This was revealed to me in the process of unlearning those three toxic beliefs and recognizing that a woman at home in her body is a threat against a system built on holding othered bodies down. A woman at peace with herself is the embodiment of the Divine Feminine. A woman who lives her truth and her healing is the Goddess incarnate. In fact, this is not just true about women, but anybody finding wholeness and healing within themselves. Which, of course, is why people who choose this path are feared. We represent the possibility of change, of living a soulful life that runs counter to mainstream culture. That's what makes us transgressive. That's what makes us radical.

And that is pure magic.

Self-Care Principles I've Had to Relearn

As I look back on my journey into radical self-care, I've learned several important things about taking care of myself. It wasn't always easy, and, in truth, I wasn't consistently great about maintaining my radical self-care goals. Why? Life happened. Real talk: thinking about self-care versus actively, aggressively cultivating it in the midst of tending to work, family life, and the inevitable curveballs the Universe sends your way are two *very* different things. All in all, I've found that it's worth putting in the time and effort to building a healthier lifestyle; even when I got off-track, I learned more about the importance of setting boundaries and letting go of things that don't enhance my overall happiness.

I also learned that being full of energy is seductive—it makes you feel invincible and tempts you to go right back to the habits and people that made you so unhappy in the first place...and then you have to begin the healing journey again when you remember why self-care was so important in the first place. Now? I'm trying to stay within the abundant joy I've conjured for myself. To trust that this happiness inside me is not finite if I continue to tend it—and that it's mine to keep and share with whomever I choose. To do that, I've had to learn three very important lessons.

Self-care is a Sensual Act.
Being present in my body. Learning what it needs to thrive. It's addictive. I love exercising and eating well. I love having quiet time at home to read by candlelight. I love finishing my days with a few yoga poses. I enjoy my life more and stress less about the little things. I have more energy and a playful spirit. I delight in my routine again. It is no longer an endless to-do list but a delicious ritual that keeps the magic flowing, so long as I stick to my self-care routine.

I relish the strengthening connection between the needs of my body and my soul and my mind. They are the three pillars grounding me so that I may thrive. If one falters, so too do the others. The reverse is also true: if one is stable, the others get stronger.

Self-care is too often about the number on the scale, the ideal body type (whatever that means!), the vitamins you take before bed. This is all good and well, but sometimes it can reduce self-care to an easy formula or image that aren't realistic or often achievable. This, in turn, disconnects us from our bodies and the process for self-care. We need to remember that taking care of ourselves is utterly delicious too. It was hard to focus on the joy of taking care of myself in the early stages. I had years of bad habits—bad magic—to undo. Then I slowly felt the effects of undoing old lives, old rituals: I felt good. Vibrant. Sexy. Like a heroine in a romance novel, if I want to be corny about it—which I do. In learning to care for myself, I rediscovered my inherent sensuality and the joy of feeling like I was taking care of myself.

Saying No is a Form of Self-Care.
No is a two-letter spell for happiness. Seriously, I've had to learn to say no. A lot. It was hard at first, because I didn't want to let people down, and, frankly, because I just get really excited about things and tend to overcommit. Then I realize that I am no use to anyone when I'm overworked. Worse, my self-care routine goes out the window due to lack of sleep, time, energy—you name it. It's hard to see the magic of everyday life when you're overextended.

So, I started turning down projects I knew I didn't have time for. I scaled back on social commitments to give myself more time to be quiet. I even gave myself more writing breaks so I could replenish myself through reading and daydreaming. I found, through all of this, that a part of me is addicted to being busy, as we've discussed. I've had to learn what it means to enjoy a full, healthy life without inviting in the frantic energy synonymous with that four-letter B-word.

I also had to draw some pretty serious emotional boundaries, removing myself from toxic people and situations or simply acknowledging the limits of certain relationships. It was a long time before I learned that turning away from things that drained me or made me feel bad about myself had a dramatic impact on my health—just as much as, if not more than, regular exercise and a good diet. When I was around toxic vibes, I ate and drank more to self-soothe and often felt anxious and riddled with self-doubt. Even my body hurt, locked in a constant state of tension as if trying to shape itself into armor to protect me from all the negativity. Then I started saying no to anything that made me feel bad. That's when things began to change. My body stopped aching. I was more energized, and enjoyed cooking and eating healthy foods. I had more energy for physical activity like walking and gardening. Bottom line: those toxic things were sapping me of my life force. I had to make the cut to reclaim my power.

Self-care Practices Should be Sustainable.
Self-care is hard work. When we think of self-care, we think about lighting scented candles and wrapping ourselves in fuzzy blankets for an afternoon of relaxation. And yes, sometimes self-care does look like that. But more often than not, self-care means getting up before the sun to work out because you know that is the only time you can reliably exercise. It means eating more greens and limiting sugar and carbs. Most of all, self-care is about putting yourself first in a world that romanticizes overwork and overextension, a difficult thing to learn if you are used to people-pleasing. It's about crafting healing routines as rituals to conjure better health.

But self-care practices also need to be sustainable. I will never be a hardcore gym rat or give up the delights of a good slice of homemade cherry pie. I won't ever fast or force myself to exercise on the days my body feels too tired. And yes, I very much look forward to a glass of wine with dinner. I needed to be realistic about what I could commit to day-in, day-out when it came to developing a self-care practice. If I got too rigid or severe in any of those practices, from diet to exercise, I would quickly backslide because the pressure to conform to those extremes was too much. But walking a little every day, spending time in my garden, and cooking meals with whole foods—those were wellness practices I could not only sustain, but actively enjoy. So now when I'm considering adding a self-care practice to my routine, I ask myself if it is sustainable. If not, I don't waste my time on it.

The definition of self-care is always evolving. Part of keeping the magic flowing is growing into new ways of tending yourself and those you love. The deeper I go into self-care, the more I let go of energies that no longer serve me and embrace the healthy things that do. They are often gentle, more holistic ways of approaching health that help me stay connected to myself. The more open I am to my self-care journey—and it is a journey, with many ups and downs—the more I'm able to find a deeper way of living.

After focusing on these important aspects of self-care, I began to understand that what I was doing when I nourished my mind, body, and soul was delving deep into the wisdom and power of the Divine Feminine. I was literally calling out to the Goddess Within and asking her to manifest in my life.

Invoking the Goddess Within Through Radical Self-Care

I first noticed this profound Divine Feminine energy calling to me after a series of synchronicities that reminded me of the importance of self-care. The first thing that happened was that after an amazing (and incredibly busy) first week back teaching, I started the long weekend feeling under the weather. I had every intention of doing everything from attending wine festivals, to dancing late into the night, to any other shenanigans that came my way. But I had only just been saying, in light of my fuller-than-usual schedule this term, that I needed to be sure to make self-care a priority. It seemed that life took over, so I had to follow through with my statement. There was no doubt about it—I felt a cold coming on. The only thing I could do was rest and relax until it went away. I literally had no choice but to take care of myself.

So, I rested. I took long naps and did gentle yoga and drank copious amounts of tea. And it was delicious. It was three whole days of cooking healthy meals inspired by farmer's market finds and indulging in afternoons reading trashy books. It made me realize how little attention I had been paying to my internal life. Then the Universe kept speaking to me in synchronous code.

The second synchronous event came when I learned that the first Sunday of that September was World Goddess Day. Trust me. It's a thing. The more I read about it, the more I loved the idea of devoting the day to Goddess energy so as to cultivate it year-round. In such a male-centric society, one that values extroversion, logic, and concrete accomplishments, Goddess energy reminds us of the equally important need to nourish introversion and tend our emotional and psychic lives.

The unfolding work weeks were spent in equal measures of sleep and homey nourishment simply because I had no energy for anything else. During this dormant time, a funny thing started to happen. I was seeing Goddess wisdom all over the place. In my newsfeed. On TV. In books. Even in my tarot deck. She was everywhere. I began to think the Universe was trying to tell me something. I was being reminded of the power of the feminine, the power of quiet and simple pleasures, the power of home as medicine. Such is the way of synchronicity.

After I tuned back into my own magic, I realized that it is too easy to forget to care for ourselves, too easy to lose track of the big picture as we navigate our day to day, too easy to dismiss pleasurable things as unimportant. We all have things we have to get done, after all. But the Goddess Within reminds us that we can be a boss in our outer daily lives and still nourish our internal lives. I needed tender things those few weeks, gentle things and beautiful things to restore myself. I needed to read fun books and lighten my energy. And I needed to imbue my home with the delicious essence of divinely beautiful living.

So, who is the Goddess Within? She is the one who rises above the daily debris that might weigh us down—she shows us the big picture of life so we don't get stuck on the small mundanities.

She is sensuous and beautiful, at home in her body. She loves to indulge in the pleasures of life. She doesn't hesitate to care for herself, as we so often do in a world that seems to demand more and more of us. She is at home with her emotions and the psychic world. In short, she is pure magic.

When we think of self-care as a way to access Goddess energy, we can begin to see ourselves as more than just a body. We become pure energy, pure consciousness that manifests itself in our physical person. Once I found her, I wanted the Goddess in all aspects of my life. Life became a sensuous, hedonistic experience the more I opened up to her, so much so that I made it a point to welcome her into all aspects of my life so that I could feel the joy of the Divine Feminine, within and without. There are three key ways to invoking this luscious goddess energy in your life.

Invite the Goddesses into Your Home.
I'm a huge proponent of making your home a sanctuary, not just a place to crash at the end of the day. I like to invoke the archetypal forces of goddesses like Aphrodite, Athena, and Demeter to decorate my sacred space. Take Aphrodite's lead and make your bedroom a sensuous space for dreaming and delighting. Make your bathroom reflect the sea-kissed shores from which she was birthed. Allow Demeter to fill your kitchen with the harvest's abundance, and Athena to make your writing desk or home office a celebration of imagination and intellectual curiosity. The more you cultivate goddess wisdom within your space, the more you feel inspired to make each act within those spaces deliberate and joyful. A sanctuary is your way of showing yourself that you are valued and that you deserve to live in a warm, vibrant space. You'll be surprised how much this influences your mental and emotional health.

Love Your Body.
Each curve, each scar, each freckle. Love it all. And treat it right. Exercise and stretch and wear clothes that fit well. Enjoy the sensuous pleasures of satin jammies. Slather it in body butter and soak your hair in honey. We are inundated with images of airbrushed bodies on magazines and other media, and advice on how to reshape ourselves into an ideal form of beauty—it's usually thin, white, and unblemished. It's important to remember that health and happiness override a certain dress size. I mean, look at Botticelli's Aphrodite: big hips, small breasts, round belly. Hardly fulfilling today's thin beauty ideals, but she's the *goddess of love and beauty.* Take your cues from her and recognize that beauty comes in all different shapes and sizes. And while you're at it, remember that beauty standards are often racist, gendered, ableist, and shaped by a ton of other toxic *-isms.* There's no such thing as self-care without self-love. Ditch the negative self-talk and instead worship your body as the beautiful vessel it is.

Protect Your You Time.
The Goddess Within is tender and playful, sure, but she's a warrior too—remember Athena. It can be hard to say no or be done working for the day. We live in a culture that can slowly start demanding more and more of us. As minorities, especially, we can struggle to draw important boundaries that lead to a more balanced life. So, invoke the warrior! Say no to things. Carve out space for what brings you joy and get comfortable establishing limits. Loving the Goddess Within doesn't mean your energy is limitless. It means that you know how to replenish yourself and create space for simply being. The energy can't flow if you don't open up the pathways.

In short, radical self-care creates Goddess energy. All magic comes from tending yourself mentally, emotionally, spiritually, and physically. You can't manifest anything without a strong foundation. Better still: your ability to conjure becomes an integral part of your identity, more intrinsic to your day-in, day-out, so much so that you often won't have to think consciously about the good magic you are cultivating.

Questions to ask yourself:

> *Is it sustainable?*
> *Does it bring me joy?*
> *What parts of myself do I need to nourish?*

Routine as Ritual: Building Self-Care into Your Day

Start Small.
It can be hard when you first immerse yourself in the routine of self-care. There's so much to change. It's tempting to go to extremes with diet, exercise, and overall lifestyle changes. The problem with that is those radical changes are not sustainable. This is especially true if you're trying to break long-term bad habits—the idea of cutting something off cold turkey is super intimating, which makes backsliding easier. So, start small. For me, it was committing to twenty minutes of yoga a day, then thirty-minute walks. Once those things felt like second nature, I began to look at diet: cutting down portion sizes and opting for more veggies and unprocessed foods. I also made little tweaks to my routines, like making a point to brew a cup of herbal tea before sleep to enjoy while I read, instead of continuing to watch TV and flopping into bed when I was too tired to watch anything anymore. All these little changes add up, and the more little adjustments you make, the easier the next one becomes.

Embrace the Process.
It's a good idea to see the early days of your self-care routine development as a form of research or data collecting. There will be quite a bit of trial and error as you learn what works best

for you and your needs. Treat this time as a form of ritual, a time when you can get to know yourself on a deeper level. For example, I used to try to push myself to make it to the gym four or five days a week—typically in the wee hours of the morning, because that was often the only time I could get it in. It went okay until the middle of the semester hit. I was overwhelmed with trying to teach, make it to the gym, and squeeze in some extra rest. I finally threw in the towel and decided that I could get an extra hour of sleep if I worked out at home. I still got up earlier to do yoga, and then incorporated more walking and movement throughout my day. Although it seemed l like I was exercising less, I actually became fitter and more rested, because this was a routine I could commit to even when my life got very full. Plus, the morning yoga gave me the much needed quiet and centering time I needed before entering my more extroverted teaching life. Still, I wouldn't have known the gym life wasn't for me unless I tried. This research ritual makes me feel confident, even today, in the self-care choices I've made.

Breathe.

Throughout the day, take a moment to breathe and check in with yourself. I like to do this around mid-afternoon, or any time I feel my energy shift. I take a deep breath, pause, and let my energy settle. Then I think about why the shift happened. Did I run into someone with manic, frazzled energy? Did I get a concerning email? Was I simply in need of a brisk walk around campus to revive my senses? Whatever the cause, checking in with myself has allowed me to see how I intuitively respond to people and situations throughout my day. This is vital information, telling me how best to avoid negative energy and cultivate healthy vibes. I reconnect with myself and let go of anything that compromises my peace. As the yogis say, breathe in the good, exhale the bad. This is also a great exercise for when you just need to reconnect, however briefly, to your internal life. Part of radical self-care is listening to your inner voice, which can so often get silenced by the noise of the outer world. So, take a deep breath, listen to your own beating heart, and find your center.

Everyday Conjuring: Welcoming in Healing Energy

Create a Space in Your Home That is Just for Self-care.
It can be as small as the space it takes to roll out a yoga mat, or as big as a room. Fill it with things that you find healing, like plants, crystals, books, essential oils, whatever works for you. This is a way to invite the Goddess into your home. When you carve out a space for healing, you welcome in powerful cleaning energy into your space. In this case, think of it as inviting the Greek goddess of healing, Panacea, into your home and body. Cure-alls, or magical elixirs that have the power to heal anything and everything, were named after this goddess, so as you build your space, think about the things you need in order to conjure magical healing energy into your life. These can be physical, like fresh flowers, or metaphysical, like words of phrases you want to meditate on. Keep this space free from anything having to do with work or other duties. For example, my bedroom is a work-free zone, strictly for relaxing, sleeping, and indulging in the finer pleasures of life (*wink wink*). This way, I always know that when I enter that room, I am entering a sanctuary that is just for my rest and rejuvenation. Plan to spend at least twenty minutes a day in your chosen sanctuary. This can be to meditate, read, stretch, or anything else that just makes you feel well. This will help you begin to see your whole home as a self-care space.

Let Your Body and Instincts Guide You.
Every morning, I like to check in with myself. I start by tuning into my body—the aches and pains, the delicious feeling of a good stretch and a well-rested mind. If something is off, I can send healing energy to it to restore balance. If I feel that my

shoulders are tight and hurting, for example, I can acknowledge that I might be trying to shoulder too much (see how the body and spirit work together to tell us things?). I can then work on opening up my shoulders and set my intention on doing less that day. Similarly, I let my intuition guide me. If something sounds instinctively fun, I give it a try. If it seems good on paper but leaves me with a nauseous feeling in the pit of my stomach, then it's a no-go. Listening to the non-verbal messages can guide you to places and people that are more in alignment with your higher vibration.

Get Used to Saying No.
I know I mentioned this earlier, but it bears repeating. It's powerful, that word. It's a two-letter spell for happiness. And like all good magic, the more you practice, the better you get at it. Committing to shamelessly eradicating toxic stress is practical magic at its best. Get comfortable drawing this basic boundary, strategically invoking Goddess fire energy. Don't apologize. Don't make long-winded excuses. Just make it clear that you can't commit to another project, social event, or other activity. Your time is your own. You don't owe anybody more of yourself than it's healthy to give.

I want to emphasize this especially for women of color and other minorities, whose time and labor are too often exploited without adequate compensation. You are not required to burn yourself out in your social justice work. You are not required to carry the emotional burdens society wants you to shoulder. You are not required to overwork to constantly prove your value. Goddess energy reminds us that self-care is a form of social justice. Valuing your own need for health and healing helps to change the narrative for minority groups from trauma and overwork to joy and balance.

If people don't understand why you've worked this two-letter spell in the first place, then they don't belong in your life.

Period. That's the tough love of saying no—you have to be firm with yourself and others. But the results are worth it. You'll free up more time and space for you to nourish yourself and to welcome things that will truly enhance your quality of life. You'll also find like-minded people on their own healing journeys who will reciprocate the energy you put into the relationship. Again, trust your instincts here. I don't care how good it sounds or if everyone is doing it—if it feels bad to you, get rid of it. We don't have unlimited energy. The power of the Goddess is in deciding what we want to do with the energy we have. My advice? Leave time to dream. Dreams, after all, are seeds that eventually sprout.

Chapter 3

Make Your Routine a Ritual

You know how it goes. It's the end of the day. You're tired. You want to put on some pajamas and veg out in front of the TV, but there's laundry to do and dinner to cook. You'd like to go for a walk or maybe take a few minutes to look at your latest sewing project, but you just don't have the energy. And that's okay. We go through cycles. Sometimes we have high-energy periods, while other times are less productive. But when we fall into a rut—go to work, crash when you get home, roll out of bed and start the cycle all over again—we have a problem. We've lost our basic connection to soul, to self.

It's like being on autopilot, where you don't have to think or even completely engage with the world around you. You begin to numb yourself and disconnect from the things that bring you joy. Most terrifying of all? You don't even realize it is happening. Without knowing it, you've become a living zombie.

The good news is that there's still a beating heart inside of you, eager to taste the simple pleasures inherent in our daily life. We just need to dust off the grave dirt—and kick the mindless habits that bring us only fleeting, superficial comfort. You know the ones I'm talking about: tucking into less-than-healthy takeout, zoning out in front of any kind of screen, ignoring the fact that your living room needs a good vacuuming...all the little things that bring a sense of immediate relief but no real long-term vitality. What your heart needs is what the rest of you needs: to slow down, unplug, and be more deliberate with your time and energy.

That's the power of making your day-in, day-out routines into rituals. They are no longer bits of drudgery you have to muscle through before you can hit the couch, but deliberate acts to conjure a wonderful life. It does require giving up those short-term comforts—comforts with diminishing returns—consciously breaking free from the shackles of mindless consumption, and embracing mindful enjoyment.

I know I've mentioned screens a few times here as things that zombify us, but I'm not saying throw out your television or other electronics. I'm no stranger to the bliss of a good movie or show on the weekend. I also love my many online communities. But what I am suggesting is slowing down and truly enjoying those things instead of using them as a form of mind-numbing medication. When you allow yourself to unplug from anything that makes you feel heavy or stagnant, you can begin to look at your routine with new eyes. You'll even come to see that many of the things on your to-do list are actually just empty busy. Sure, laundry is a must, as is cleaning the house...but have you considered that maybe you don't need to run those thousand errands or go down that social media rabbit hole?

Unplugging from our fast-paced life and sinking into routines as rituals is about consciously slowing our minds down and tuning into what we are doing. Our bodies and schedules aren't the only things that move too fast. Think about when you lie awake at night running through your massive to-do list, even though there is nothing you can do about it at two in the morning. Things that need to get done. Things you should have said. Or the countdown to the next time you can unwind.

It's an easy trap to fall into. Even after years of meditating on my routines as powerful rituals, I can sometimes get swept up in the current of life and find myself slipping back into zombie mode. After a particularly stressful year professionally, I found myself waking each morning and counting down the hours until I could be home in my pajamas, eating pizza and shutting out the world. The problem with this, however, is that I had lost my innate sense of joy in greeting the day, the soft warmth in my belly when I unlocked my front door in the evening, and the simple delight of doing yoga or tending the garden before making an easy, healthy dinner. I'd even lost the cozy bliss of a cup of tea and a good book before bed—I was too tired to bother putting the kettle on. In the stress of what I was working through, I'd forgotten to connect to myself.

And as we know from the first two chapters, connection to self is the first and most important step to cultivating everyday magic. If we lose our connection to self and soul, we lose our magic. Finding our way back to ourselves includes examining our routines and the kind of energy they bring into our lives. We all follow a routine. Some of them are good (exercising regularly), some of them are bad (hitting that snooze button one too many times). When we view these rote tasks as something meaningful, however, we have to be more thoughtful about the kind of life we want to live.

Making your routine a ritual forces you to live more intentionally and be conscious of the energy you're bringing into your home and conjuring in your life. So, stop pushing the snooze button so you can get up and do your morning yoga. Hard at first, I know, but so worth it when you go through your day feeling soft and flexible, like a tree bending in the wind. Resist the temptation for another round of takeout and instead slow down and enjoy a simple home-cooked meal. It doesn't have to be fancy, just yummy. Fill your day with little things that make you happy and nourish your soul.

There may even be room in your routine-as-ritual for a little takeout and an occasional snooze-button tapping. But the bulk of your day-in, day-out should be things that contribute to your overall sense of wellness. I think about how I want to start and end the day and what I need to do to feel refreshed for the next day, and plan my routine around that. I avoid any patterns that feel old and stale or make me feel heavy. I commit to rituals that make me feel connected to myself and give me an overall sense of well-being. When you cultivate intentional living, the magic flows freely.

The Difference Between Routine and Ritual

According to the Oxford English Dictionary, routine is defined as "a sequence of actions regularly followed." Pretty straightforward. It's the stuff we do regularly, without fail, whether they are good for us (taking a short walk to revive your senses at work) or bad (always hitting the vending machine at three in the afternoon). Some are more mundane: pay the rent at the first of the month, take your six-month visit to the dentist, get an oil change and lube for your car. We are so used to these things as basic parts of adult life that we never really think too hard about them unless something is out of joint (not sure how you will pay your rent, a sketchy dentist, weird noises coming from your car's engine). Hell, our routines are so ingrained, we often zone out while doing them. Have you ever driven home from work via the same route you take every day and had no memory of the drive? That's you on autopilot. Your routine is so second-nature you disconnect from the actual activity you're doing.

The second definition of routine is equally telling. It defines it as "a set sequence in a performance such as a dance or comedy act." So routine is not just a basic repetitive schedule, but something we *perform*, consciously or unconsciously. I know this definition specifically deals with routine in terms of artistic performances, but I don't think it's a stretch to consider our daily lives as a type of song and dance, if you will. It's all about how we want people to see us. Running from one thing to the next practically shouts that we are busy, interesting, important! It also broadcasts our values. Do you value squeezing in one more thing at work over finishing a few minutes early and heading home to enjoy some leisurely self-care? Do you pack your weekends with activities and experiences, or do you create time to dally? Each decision shapes how we see ourselves and how others see us. But these definitions of routine only take us so far—only far enough to get us thinking about how we see ourselves and how we want others to see us. But what about what we want to feel, experience, and enjoy?

That's where ritual comes in. Ritual is about consciously, mindfully tending to our daily tasks, taking comfort in their familiarity and pleasure in how they ground and nurture us. We welcome the healthy and the good and actively eliminate the life-diminishing and bad. In order to do that, however, we have to change how we look at our day-in, day-out. It's not a place we need to escape from. It's not a collection of minutes that fills our time until the real fun—a weekend, celebration, or happy event—begins. It's about finding joy in the life we create for ourselves, one small, deliberate act at a time. I'm reminded of the Ten of Cups in the tarot here—the homey gratitude card that asks you to step back and appreciate all the simple magic of your life that you've worked hard to create.

The first step to unplugging from rote activities and mindless routine is to find enjoyment in the things we often perceive as One More Thing To Do. Celebrate chores, rather than dreading them, by turning them into rituals that help you unplug from your workday and reconnect with yourself. So, I have to turn my compost—good. Dirt in my fingernails grounds me and feeding the worms connects me to nature. So, I don't know what to cook for dinner—I'll start with sautéing an onion and let my farm-fresh ingredients speak to me. Taking the extra time to cook a healthy meal allows me to nourish my whole being and enjoy the quiet hedonism of sautéing vegetables. Time in the kitchen allows me to slow down and reconnect to the deliciousness that is life. Throw in a jazz record and a glass of wine, and you've got the makings of a divine evening. Now, doesn't that sound lovely?

Each and every task becomes a devotional act to the energy I want to welcome into my life and an expression of gratitude for the abundance I have painstakingly cultivated. A celebration of my hard work and a deliberate conjuring of more good energy.

Routines I've Had to Unlearn

I love that my routines are rituals now. I feel a deep sense of satisfaction and calm—but it took me time to get there. For starters, I had to rethink much of what mainstream culture teaches us about our daily life: Day-in, day-out is boring. My job is just a paycheck. Fun happens someplace else. The sad reality of these ideas is that they set you up for a pretty non-magical life...and a depressing one, too. I recognized routine as a powerful form of everyday conjuring once I let go of these three useless—no, *toxic*—concepts.

Mundane is Boring.

Ever notice how people respond when asked what they did over the weekend? Sometimes the answer is full of action-packed excitement that seems to show just how much that person is living life to the fullest. Most times, however, the responses range from staying home and chilling out to running errands and taking care of house stuff. The less glamorous answers are always given, of course, with a sheepish, down-cast glance, as if their life is boring if they aren't off in pursuit of the next big adventure. We're taught early on that if we aren't living our lives like we're characters in a summer blockbuster, we aren't truly fulfilling our potential of happiness.

Here's the thing, though. I love—I mean *love*—a good putter around the house. You know the kind. When you don't have any set plans for your Saturday but end up cleaning out some old drawers or sifting through your crafting project piles (we all have those, right?). I love running the occasional simple errand too—to the grocery store, in particular—and leaving time for a good nap if I can get it, not to mention some time to read, write, and cook. And while sometimes throwing caution to the wind and adventuring is fun, I find I need quieter weekends to tend to the things I can't during the week. This doesn't mean I'm always at home. It just means I do quieter things with a handful of people that I don't often advertise.

And yes, a lot of the time you can find me at home, puttering. Playing with herbs. Cooking. Cleaning. Napping with my cat. None of it is especially glamorous on paper but, given the choice between an afternoon drinking tea and reading and the next big bucket-list-worthy escapade, I'll take a few hours with a good book any time. I can say that with the certainty of someone who did say yes to all the next-big-things for about a year just to see if I was, indeed, missing out. The truth? I wasn't. Worse, those things made me feel disconnected from myself, because I had lost the space and time for reflection.

There's another important aspect of embracing the art of the ritualized routine. Something devastating and profound. Embracing mundane enjoyments means having to let go of preconceived notions of what *living* actually means, not to mention giving up the addiction to empty extroversion. We move fast so that we don't have to hear ourselves. In short, when we let go of all the things we think we should be doing for fear of missing out, and allow ourselves to just be—even if *just being* means doing laundry—all sorts of feelings and thoughts come out that need to be processed. Some are intense, even painful, but they are important all the same. In my years of magical living, I've come to learn that we are afraid of slowness, quiet, and mundane activities precisely for the reasons we need them. They offer us space to breathe, process, and learn who we are at our most basic level.

Mundane is no longer boring to me. It's a meditation to travel the same roads and learn yourself each day with each pattern you tend.

Monday is a Four-letter Word.
I often say that Monday is the ugly duckling of the weekday. But to be honest, I've never understood that. I love diving into a Monday after a restful weekend, ready to greet the work

week and take new challenges and opportunities. Why? I see Mondays as the clean slate. The open road. And, yes, the homey comfort of a bowl of green chile stew and a pot of tea at the end of the day.

Part of its reputation stems from the idea that we have to squeeze in fun on weekends and evenings, but if you are living a life of intentional ritual, you come to learn that enjoyment comes in experiencing each day to its fullest expression. That includes heartaches or setbacks as well as the delights and miracles of the day—feeling what you need to feel is an integral part of everyday magic. Feeling stressed on Sunday night? It's usually a sign that you're taking on too much at work or needing to set boundaries. If you listen to the feeling, you can find a solution. Sometimes the simple act of being aware of the things causing you pain is enough to help you begin to find a way to mend. In either case, Monday isn't an ugly duckling—it's a fresh start. Let it guide you towards new inspiration.

Life Would Be So Much Better/Easier/More Fun If...
Who hasn't fantasized about running off to a different country to live "the good life?" I certainly have on more than one occasion, when work got stressful or life hectic. It was a long-standing joke for me in graduate school that one of these days I would run away to Tuscany and write bodice-rippers . . . but that was before I learned that I could do that right where I was—or where I ended up, back in the Land of Enchantment. Happiness is where you cultivate it.

You see, I learned that location is a state of mind. That is, my writing career (to eventually include said romances) was something that I could make happen anytime, anywhere. It wasn't dependent on leaving my here and now any more so that it was on fleeing the country. It was about the energy I brought to my everyday life. I owe this bit of wisdom, in part, to the many wonderful people I know who became ex-pats to pursue their writing and artistic careers free from the shackles of Real Life. Guess what? Turns out, their life is just as rich and complicated, and *mundane,* as mine is. That escape destination goes from a fantasy to Real Life, with all its delights, surprises, and difficulties. It doesn't matter where you go or what the world throws your way, life is life, so it's best to grow and thrive like a weed: Where and how you can.

Rituals I've Had to Relearn

I've had some hard lessons to unlearn. Some difficult patterns to let go of. My dismissal of everyday life left me feeling stressed, passionless, and unhappy. Once I let go of the negative ideologies that made me dismiss everyday life, I began to appreciate its value. There, in that fertile space, I relearned a few things that made that appreciation sprout and blossom into love.

Routine is Soothing.
Tell me you haven't had a day you've enjoyed simply because it was so utterly mundane. Roasted chicken on Monday. Clean the house on Wednesday. Groceries on Thursday. Stay up late reading on Friday. The thing you do because you do it every week on that specific day. Those routines are what we begin to look forward to when we understand that they are magic.

I heal from a rough week when I putter up and down the aisle of the grocery store, thinking about what yummy thing to cook over the weekend. I find new inspiration in making the same green chile stew and tortillas I've had since I can remember helping my mom cook dinner. Then there's the dreaming. Night after night after night. A cup of tea and a half-hour of reading before submitting to the whims and wisdom of the dreamworld. All these things are soothing balms to the ups and downs of an average day.

In routine, I find myself again and again.

My Thoughts Matter.

A hard day can lead to an evening of negative thinking. All my self-doubts resurface, like old ghosts waiting for an invitation back into my home. It's too easy to slip into heavy thoughts, or pick at all the little things that made my day stressful, or dwell on ways I could have done something better. You know how it goes. I've learned to check if I'm overly tired, anymore. Old ghosts are just that: things best left in the past, like the debris of the day. And, the reality is, half the things I begin to fret over when I'm in this state are things I have no control over or are not as big of a deal as my tired mind makes them out to be.

I focus on what I enjoyed during the day. I take a moment to appreciate the ups and downs that keep me on my toes. And I give myself space to be tired, rather than feeling like I should have more energy than I do at that moment. Even the bumps and surprises become life lessons that nourish me, rather than nuisances and pains. Same goes for the chores and other mundane activities that can feel like too much when I'm tired. They become the practices that bring me back to myself. Washing dishes, fixing the sink, even cleaning out the cat litter ground me in the soothing rote quality of the task. I can let my mind wander — unwind — while I occupy my hands and body. Better still, the little mundanities that are sprinkled through the week become soothing morsels to be savored for the very fact that they ground me and offer me insight into myself and the outside world.

It's the Little Things that Make a Day Great.

The other day, I was at the local farmers' market and found a stand with the most beautiful bouquets of fresh-cut lavender. I brought some home with me to put on my nightstand and writing desk. All week, my home was perfumed with the heady summery scent of blooming purple flowers. Heaven! It was a little thing that made me happy to wake up in the morning and eager to return home to at the end of the day.

Part of turning routines into rituals is embracing the small joys of daily life. Savor them. That afternoon cup of tea. The recipe you want to try, and the grocery store visit to get the ingredients for it. We take these sacred, simple pleasures for granted (more on that in the next chapter). We should pause to absorb the pleasure they bring us and seek out more pleasures, rather than rushing through the day without pause or reflection.

Questions to ask yourself:

What negative patterns am I holding on to? Why?
What joys could I replace them with?
What do I want my daily life to feel like?

Routine as Ritual: Turning Your Routines into Meaningful Rituals

Eat Well — and Cook Your Own Meals.
It's time to let your inner kitchen witch out! Aim for fresh foods like veggies and grains. Ditch packaging. Create space for a delicious, healthy dinner at the end of the day. It doesn't have to be fancy or time-consuming. Half of my weeknight dinners are sautéed kale, sweet potatoes and garlic, roasted veggies and chicken, or a simple chile stew I can eat all week. But your dinner should, above all things, be magical. Learn to see the contents of your pantry and fridge as ingredients for healing spells. Feeling down? Nothing a little medicinal spell like green chile stew can't fix. Need to celebrate? Nopales tacos are a recipe for finding the joy in learning from prickly situations. Want a love spell? That's what chocolate-dipped strawberries are for. Minutes to prep, and while they cook, I can sink into a little yoga or water my plants. The idea is to unplug from fast living by slowing down at the end of the day. Cooking helps with that, as does

eating a healthy meal which nourishes you rather than weighing you down or numbing you out (I think we all know emotional eating is a thing). Worst-case scenario—you don't know what to cook and you're super tired—start by chopping and sautéing an onion. The aroma will put you in the mood for a satisfying meal and inspire that evening's dish. Trust me. It works every time.

Move Your Body Regularly.
Dance. Walk. Wiggle. Stretch. Weed the garden. Doesn't matter what it is, except that I commit to something every day and treat it as a sensory experience and time to reconnect to my body. I've found that it's easier to maintain if the activity is something I can incorporate fairly easily into my routine (hence gardening or walking to the store). Even when I feel at my busiest, I find that ending the day with a little body movement transforms me. I go from tired to rejuvenated. Stressed to decompressed. Totally worth it! And, yes, I know this should probably have been in my self-care chapter, but exercise of any kind is a form of moving meditation. It's a devotional practice to self and the body. Exercise becomes a sacred activity when we treat it as a daily ritual of self-care rather than an obligatory gym session.

Clean Your Home.
There's nothing like a little elbow grease and good, old-fashioned labor to clear out bad energy and dusty thoughts from your mind and home. As I always say, good housekeeping is the best cleansing spell I know. Seriously! I love the searing energy of burning sage or the soft, warm, purifying energy of beeswax candles, but those don't do a darned thing if your home isn't already clean. You'll be surprised how much clarity you gain from a fully stocked kitchen, a tidy home, and a closet full of neatly folded laundry. It's not glamorous—but it sure is magical. There's nothing more conducive to inviting everyday enchantments into your life than a clean home and an open mind.

Conjuring Everyday Magic: Opening Up to the Magic of Routine as Ritual

Start a New Ritual.
One of the easiest, and most fun, ways to begin thinking of your routines as rituals is to start a new ritual. Make it small—and special. It could be as simple as lighting a beeswax candle when you get home from work to signal the transition from day to night. Or you could block out time to read before bed—just twenty minutes—with a cup of tea and your favorite throw. One ritual I'm returning to is taking my morning coffee outside. I like to greet the day, run my fingers through my plants, and watch the sunrise. Sometimes it's only a few minutes; other times, like the weekend, I can linger. Whatever you choose, make your ritual something that's just for you. Sometimes we need to try something new in order to appreciate the everyday things we do and take for granted. You'll be surprised how you start seeing your daily routine differently with just a touch more awareness and time carved out for simple rituals.

Bookend Your Day with Small Forms of Self-Care.
These small acts of self-care should include mind, body, and soul. I'm not talking about your regular exercise, eating well, or checking on your emotional and mental health, although those are very important. Rather, now you can begin to extend your self-care routine to things that soothe and ground—remember the Goddess. Do you like to rub essential oils along your temples before bed? Or start the day with a glass of lemon water? Maybe you like to meditate or consult tarot before the sun rises. Or just set the alarm fifteen minutes earlier so you have a few extra minutes to linger in bed and ruminate on the messages from the dream world. Maybe you want to have a glass of wine and paint your nails at the end of a long workday. Whatever the case, bookending your day with these soothing moments helps you

slow down and free up your energy so that you aren't running on fumes or becoming stagnant.

Write Down Your Dream Routine.
Maybe you can't have it now, but what would it look like? Fantasies tell us a lot about the life we want, so tap into that magic and imagine what an ideal day would be for you. I'm not talking ideal vacation day. I'm talking Tuesday. What's the best possible Tuesday routine you could imagine? What do you need to do to get there?

For me, I have to write every day. Writing is one of my most sacred forms of magic. Without it, I am lost, disconnected from myself. I need it to imagine new ways of being and to remember to trust my magic. Sometimes I write for a few minutes, others longer.

Play with it—the words, the schedules, the fantasies— and think what the kind of life your ideal routine represents. In graduate school, I used to fantasize about one routine in particular so much so that it was borderline erotic for me. That routine was a quiet life of teaching, writing, living a simple life in my hometown. I would think about it down to the pot of tea ordered at my local cafe to hold me over while grading papers and the thirty-minute walk to the herb store. After years of dreaming, that routine finally bore fruit. It's the life I live now. That's how magic works: dream it up, then work towards it.

Chapter 4

Practice Pleasure Magic

Here is where things get really juicy. You've tuned into everyday magic. You've begun your journey into radical self-care and are retooling your routines to be rituals. Now it's time to revel in the pleasures of life. Pleasure magic is the invocation of all things luscious and joyful. It asks you to tune into what soothes the soul and refreshes the senses without guilt, without shame, without comparing your journey to others. Pleasure is a vital part of life. When we consciously welcome it into our daily routine, we craft a vibrant, healthy way of being.

In order to heal our relationship to pleasure, we first have to acknowledge that we live in a culture that devalues it. We're afraid of it, and religion certainly doesn't help with that. It teaches us to fear our bodies and anything that brings us joy, because happy feelings, delicious feelings, must stem from sin, right? Wrong. Pleasure is birthed from the divine, however you choose to identify it.

This negative relationship to pleasure is magnified if you are a person of color, like me, or another minority. Simply put, you unconsciously (or, sometimes, consciously) harbor feelings of *less-than,* a symptom of internalized oppression. It's the little voice that tells you that you don't deserve joy, that you are not entitled to things that make you feel good. Pleasure Magic is, then, an integral part of healing histories of colonization and generational trauma. We get to transform toxic narratives into ones of hope and healing—and, yes, pleasure. That is the Divine Feminine in all of us, healing what needs to be healed.

I view this divinity as the sacred feminine, regardless of a person's gender. Pleasure, that soft, amorphous thing, is closely linked to this goddess energy that asks us to celebrate abundance, joy, and well-being—guilt-free. One of the best ways to welcome that abundant healing energy into your life is to treat simple pleasures as sacred. Getting lost in a good story, a bouquet of flowers on your nightstand, homemade pasta, a love letter... All these things connect us to the Divine Feminine within ourselves. And let's face it: That's kind of terrifying!

What this divine delighting reveals is that we all have a profound capacity for joy, which in turn means that we are so much more than the limited narratives we've built for ourselves. Doom and gloom are easy—you just feed the beast of negativity. But bliss? It's hard work, but the payoff is real. If we can touch that sacred feminine within ourselves, even if it's only for a moment, we must confront just how much power we have to shape our lives.

I think that's why it is so easy to devalue simple pleasures as trivial things. If we make them *less-than* in the way we feel *less-than*, we never have to confront how we hold ourselves back and are complicit in our own oppression. Too often, taking a moment to breathe or indulge is seen as laziness, a lack of industry in a world that privileges concrete accomplishments and masculine extroversion. And yet, I can directly link every one of my external successes to my internal balance and joy, my connection to the sacred feminine through pleasure. Through this, I've had to acknowledge the beautiful, and yes, sometimes scary, fact that the divine is within us. That we are infinite. That we can only grow and thrive if, like plants, we let the light in.

This divine delighting is an integral part of conjuring everyday magic. It allows you to take refuge in the light of a beeswax candle and inspiration from a soft breeze tickling your skin. These quiet moments remind us that the world is more than just tasks to accomplish. In fact, pleasure tells us a lot about ourselves. It's easy to identify a toxic situation because it makes us feel so bad. But once we address negative issues, how do we then cultivate joy? It takes a lot to conjure and maintain happiness. We have to get used to what pleasure feels like and perhaps spend more time unabashedly courting its presence in our lives. Like any good reader of romance knows, the iconic happily-ever-after takes a lot of grit and hard work to achieve. We have to ask ourselves hard questions: What makes me happy? What do I want in my life? What *doesn't* bring me pleasure? Seemingly simple questions, sure, but how often are we honest with ourselves about what we enjoy, as opposed to what society tells us we should be doing?

Pleasure, then, is something that allows us to be honest about who we are and what we need to not just survive, but thrive. We also learn, through pleasure magic, how to listen to our intuition without guilt. The best way to explain this is through a little story. Time and again, I have found myself in a social situation that I committed to not because I necessarily wanted to, but because I thought I should be doing it. It seemed like a good idea, but my gut feeling told me it wasn't my vibe. There would inevitably be a lot of gossip flying around and more than a little drama. In the space of a week, I would go from being happy and full of life to tired, anxious, and without inspiration for my writing. Those feelings told me a lot. In talking with loved ones, I was finally able to trace these feelings back to stepping into a zone that wasn't right for me. Once I had that revelation, my energy returned.

I felt happy again—albeit tired from this strange emotional journey. I could write once more. I looked forward to my workday. And I felt joy in the littlest things. The energetic shift was shocking and made me realize how much I took my inner joy for granted. In reality, I became so happy because I nourished the sacred art of pleasure and eschewed anything that didn't enhance the quality of my life. It made me feel like I could do anything and everything—including return to unhealthy situations and relationships that seemed less toxic with distance. Stepping back into those dead zones showed me that wasn't the case.

My energy had been abundant because I cultivated abundance

and ruthlessly cut out anything from my life that didn't enhance my overall wellness. But when I began to doubt myself or succumb to social pressures, I lost myself. Then I'd retreat into my sanctuary to heal, replenish, feel better...and the cycle would start all over again. I repeatedly found myself in this type of situation which forced me to come to terms with the fact that I often acquiesced to social engagements out of a strange sense of anxiety and obligation—what I thought I *should* be doing— rather than any sense of actual pleasure I might take from those outings. When I do accept invites out now, I know it's because I actually want to go.

Lesson learned. That's the beauty of pleasure magic and making pleasure an integral part of your day-to-day. It helped me understand why certain things make me anxious and unhappy—and that it is okay to let those things go in favor of radical joy. Now, I should warn you that pleasure magic isn't just about basking in the glow of hedonistic delights. It isn't about never having negative feelings or never allowing yourself to engage with things that make you uncomfortable. Rather, this is about meaningfully allowing yourself to feel what you need to feel and listen to what those feelings are telling you. True, we find out a lot about ourselves from painful situations. But it is equally important to listen to what our pleasurable experiences have to teach us as well.

As much as I write about the Divine Feminine and the softer energies in our lives, I've realized just how much masculine energy I have. I'm used to being assertive and aggressive in my pursuit of what I want. But the cultivation of pleasure magic is entirely different. For one thing, the energy is much more passive than I was originally used to. I've had to cultivate openness, a receptivity which in itself felt intensely vulnerable. I'm a novice in many respects here, when I was used to being an expert. For another, I learned quickly that more people, more activities, and more out-there energy didn't necessarily invoke the sacredness of pleasure. In fact, it was the opposite: I was tired, anxious, and in need of some serious quiet time. I know some of this is overlap from other chapters, but all these aspects of everyday magic are interconnected, showing us through various perspectives how we can heal ourselves.

Through these two misconceptions about this ephemeral thing called joy—that it was a loud, performative thing and that I could access it with the same masculine energy I applied to my professional life—I quickly learned that I had to change my relationship to pleasure. In truth, I found that pleasure was found in the simplest of things—morning walks, sipping iced tea on my patio, a schedule-free Sunday, the magic of a good book. They didn't cost money or company to bring me pleasure. The more I made time for those things, the more I began to think of them as sacred. They gave me so much, after all, and allowed me to explore parts of myself that had long been dormant.

A lot of different emotions came up in the process of reclaiming these sacred simple pleasures—not all of them pleasant. I had to come to terms with the fact that I had denied myself certain pleasures or suppressed parts of myself to fit into mainstream extroverted culture and survive in white spaces. In was in a constant state of protecting myself, and, as a result, I kept a lot of good things out too. The fear of being vulnerable kept me from my fullest expression of happiness. There is pleasure in these epiphanies too, however bittersweet. They allow me to acknowledge my past limitations so I can move forward unshackled. In essence, pleasure magic allows you to safely process sorrows and heartbreaks, wounds and traumas, with the knowledge that there is hope, hope in the form of the freedom of experiencing joy.

There was one phrase that kept coming to mind as I worked through the difficult emotions my pleasure magic unearthed: To allow. It'd been popping up all over the place. What am I allowed energetically, emotionally, physically? Or, put more accurately, what have I allowed myself to enjoy? The painful epiphany that emerged from these questions was that I haven't allowed myself to enjoy certain things, without even realizing that I'd drawn a line in the sand. It's a subtle thing—telling yourself you have to work instead of watching the sunset, letting stress taint your thoughts because you can't possibly be this happy, being stingy with your fun because there are so many other things you should be doing. Hell, I didn't even know I was doing it half the time until I started making a conscious effort to create space for non-goal-oriented pleasure.

Much of this comes from the cultural shame surrounding pleasure. If it feels good, mainstream religion tells us, it must be bad. Think of the Puritanical roots of white America. If it is enjoyable, it's certainly the seed of sin, it cautions us. Worst of all, I've realized that the fear of pleasure is a fear of happiness. We spend so much time worrying about whether we will get our HEA (Happily Ever After) that we never stop to think about how much it terrifies us. We wonder, secretly, if we are capable of holding so much joy.

So how do we tap into sacred simple pleasures, with the myriad of feelings they unleash? Simple. Dive in. Without thought or questions. Unfettered by the fear of our own infinite potential for happiness. Be sinful. Shamelessly enjoy the small pleasures you have denied yourself in your own unconscious attempt to put a limit on happiness. Welcome in bigger pleasures, too. Find just one little thing you enjoy and revel in it. The magic will follow. Once you do, you can begin to welcome in Eros energy.

Reclaiming Pleasure as Sacred with Eros Energy

A few years ago, I experienced a swirl of synchronous happenings, all of which were centered on the myth of Psyche and Eros. There was the Facebook post about walking through our private underworlds in order to find our way to Eros and, ultimately, the hard work it takes to cultivate happiness. Then there were the articles I stumbled across on the Divine Eros and freeing our Eros energy. That's not even getting into the daily signs that crossed my path, from candles and cupids to seeds and golden thread.

Most of these signs might be easily dismissed by the simple fact that Valentine's Day was around the corner (when scented candles and cupid-shaped chocolates abound), if not for the fact that I saw these things in unexpected places, not in holiday store displays. The seeds came to me from an unlikely place: a random gift of my favorite popcorn, lovingly stored in a mason jar, and a forgotten bag of seeds I'd harvested the previous summer tucked into my junk drawer, calling to mind Psyche sorting seeds in the first of many trials set by Aphrodite. The glittery sweater that I found in the back of my closet was reminiscent of the golden wool Psyche had to collect to prove her love for Eros. There was even more than one dream about navigating Hell or wading through choppy waters, two more trials Psyche endured. It seemed after I read that Facebook post, all I could see were signs of this Eros energy.

Clearly, the Universe was trying to tell me something. And when the Universe speaks, I listen. My task, it seemed, was to reconnect to Eros in my quest to deepen my relationship to the sacredness of simple pleasures. Eros energy isn't just about romantic love or eroticism, it's about reconnecting to the passionate energy within ourselves, trusting the joy we inhabit rather than doubting it, as Psyche did when she was at first convinced her lover, Eros, was a monster in her bed. Eros energy is the lifeblood of our daily lives, the healthy relationality with ourselves and others that makes life delicious. We are all like Psyche, in one way or another, doing the hard work to reclaim our private paradises. We travel through our proverbial hells and complete seemingly endless trials to reclaim our natural, passionate essence, unblemished by experience, outside voices (which caused Psyche to doubt her love in the first place), and our own uncertainty.

So, life was telling me something: I had to work my way back to the earthy hedonism, the everyday eroticism you feel when you are at peace with yourself, in union with the things that make you feel happy, healthy, whole. I'd lately felt disconnected from myself, operating more out a sense of obligation than actual enjoyment, fearful of turning down social obligations because I didn't want to offend anyone. In truth, I wanted to be home; I needed to be quiet. I needed to slow down after some time of feeling like I was moving increasingly faster and faster. I didn't feel joyful or lusty for life. I felt tired—and it was only the beginning of the year. Somewhere between holiday break and beginning teaching again, I had stopped listening to myself, stopped connecting to Eros.

In order to find my way back to my Eros energy, I had to ask myself hard questions—what really brings me joy? —and be honest about my answers, which were, frankly, counter to the social norm. I thought of Psyche as I worked on opening up myself to the love vibes. I thought of her separating seeds: What intentions do I want to plant? What do I need to feel nourished? How can I find my golden moments without climbing an uphill battle to get to them? Again, I looked to Psyche, gathering golden fleece left on the reeds the rams brushed against, rather than confront these dangerous animals head-on. There are gentler ways of doing things.

Then we must not forget the waters of forgetfulness. Psyche bringing a jug of those waters back to Aphrodite is not to erase the past but to let go of the petty details and small grievances that only weighed her down. You can't hold on to everything, or you've no room for present happiness. Her journey to the Underworld reminds me that I can't give energy to things that drain me, just as Psyche must remain focused on the road ahead of her and not be distracted by the lost souls that call to her.

All well and good. But what does finding your way back to

Eros look like when you are an ordinary human? Much the same as Psyche's journey, truthfully. I saturated my senses with things that made me feel inordinately happy. I conjured Eros's fire to illuminate my path. I sorted seeds and gathered golden threads. I stopped giving energy to things that drained me as I move into a new phase of my life. I gave myself more quiet time so that I could listen to myself, my needs. And yes, there may have been one or two heart-shaped chocolates and lighted candles.

Lest this seem all too easy, consider how we, as a culture, shy away from what we really want (such as people-pleasing) and unadulterated pleasure (surely, we must always be working). It can be a difficult journey to find our way to joy, to passionate pleasure in all things. But it's so worth it.

Lessons I've Had to Unlearn to Open Myself to Sacred Simple Pleasures

Pleasure will always be one of those deeply intimate, ephemeral things. A healthy relationship to pleasure in all its forms— physical, emotional, psychological, and spiritual—deepens our relationship to ourselves and increases our capacity for meaningful connections with others. Like all forms of magic, sinking into the sacredness of simple pleasures means we experience a great deal less of surface-life, surface-relationships, but are rewarded with better, if fewer, relationships and a slower, more enchanted way of living. To do that, however, requires a complete rejection of mainstream culture's obsessive need to regulate our passions and pleasures.

My Ability to Experience Pleasure is Finite.

We can be so stingy with our profound capacity for joy, as if afraid we might run out of this energetic sunshine. But the truth is, it's like a muscle. The more we cultivate an enjoyment of sacred, simple pleasures, the more we open ourselves to things that feel good, the stronger our capacity for pleasure gets. The hard part in all this is that we can feel vulnerable opening ourselves to overwhelming emotions, as they make us feel exposed. It can seem like a weakness to be that open, but it's not. It's an integral part of strengthening our sense of self and our right to a fulfilling life. The more we realize that opening ourselves to happiness is not the same thing as opening ourselves to all things—including the bad—the easier it is to joyfully cultivate healthy boundaries.

Opening ourselves to our infinite ability to experience pleasure helps us nourish the dream lifestyle we've always wanted. We learn not just what is toxic to us, but what sets our soul on fire— and how to protect that abundant energy. It's one thing to know that you're unhappy, feeling stuck, or that certain situations are no good for you. It's quite another to experience Eros energy. Once you do, you're driven to protect it. And as you protect it, you find it in the simplest of things: a ladybug crawling along a tree branch, a bumper crop of lemon balm, cat whiskers against your cheek first thing in the morning (the only alarm clock, other than the finches' singing, that you'll ever need).

There's No Such Thing as Pleasure Without Guilt.
Guilt is overrated, especially when it comes to pleasure. I can't believe how long it took me to relearn this. I used to feel guilty taking time for myself. Guilty that I liked "trashy" novels, from romances and gothic tales to sword and sorcery and monster hunter fiction. Guilty that I wanted my life to be more magical— that I dared to wish for more. *Don't be greedy,* a little voice inside my head would whisper. *You have enough. Don't expect too much of anything or anyone.* Don't even get me started about what that voice said about my taste in literature, or the times I sheepishly disappeared from the hustle and bustle of life to relish quiet time in the kitchen or garden, soaking up the sweet sound of silence. In fact, I realized that I thought of all my simple pleasures as *guilty pleasures* because of the fundamental shame I felt when I allowed myself to enjoy them.

I've since learned to squash that voice. There's nothing wrong with enjoying stories that inspire me to live with more magic, welcome in Eros energy, and banish a ghost or two. My guilt in taking care of myself, or even acknowledging that I am, in fact, a hard-core introvert, has since been replaced by the deep well of contentment I feel when I allow myself to be who I am and enjoy what I enjoy. Guilt—that ugly, pernicious thing—is merely a tool of toxic white patriarchy, designed to make me hate myself and thus make me more manageable.

Frankly, I'd rather be a wild brown woman who reads trashy novels past her bedtime. A wild brown woman who prefers the company of trees and garden plants to too many people. A wild brown woman who can find magic in the littlest of joys. It's more fun that way.

I Have to Suffer.
When you're used to oppression or having your existence regulated by mainstream culture, a strange thing can start happening, even as you consciously work your way out from under those toilsome ideologies. You can find little ways to make yourself suffer, if you feel like you are just a little too happy. It's everyday gothic in action. We get spooked by how much we are growing with some sunshine. We become afraid that this feeling can't last, as we relearn that our ability to experience pleasure is infinite. We might also worry that this much bubbly energy draws the wrong kind of attention our way—envy, or *el mal ojo*, the evil eye—so we dull ourselves down a bit to stay safe. We take the wind out of our own sails before anyone else can. Sick, right?

When these feelings of *less-than* surface, I slow down, tune into what stirred them up in the first place. It's usually because I've been enjoying myself quite a bit that I panic a little. What if I can't sustain this joy? What if someone will come along and make me feel bad about it? Why should such a basic thing like finding cactus for nopales tacos at my local market make me so happy? The answer to all those questions is the same: it doesn't matter. What matters is that I take the risk to let the light in.

Lessons I've Had to Relearn to Fully Relish Sacred Simple Pleasures

Relearning the sacredness of simple pleasures had a lot to do with letting go of feelings of guilt and inadequacy. Relearning to fully relish these pleasures is all about being shameless in my pursuit of what makes me feel my freest, truest self. It's a little scary, yes, but that's the price for a more magical life. You wouldn't think that cultivating sacred simple pleasures is hard work, but it is. It requires time and attention to actively nourish those things and, as a result, welcome more of that loving Eros energy into your life. Part of relearning the joy of simple pleasures is appreciating the hard work it has taken to unlearn toxic systems that told me I am not allowed to be healthily hedonistic.

I Deserve Pleasure.
This has become something of a meditation or spell for me. It is nothing short of a radical proclamation. Each and every time I say it, I banish internalized oppression and *less-than* feelings. One thing that has helped me feel empowered to reclaim my right to pleasure is letting go of comparing my journey to others'. Some might be more naturally aware of their divine right to joy, while others intrinsically have various privileges that enable and prioritize their right to pleasure over that of minority bodies. Still others have spent longer than me relearning their innate capacity for pleasure. Whatever the case, I've come to celebrate my journey as its own simple pleasure: The ups and downs, the revelations that emerge as I open myself to a gentler way of life. The sweetness that comes from allowing myself to experience the finer things in life.

It is a soft, bittersweet feeling to understand the ways I've

· kept this delight from myself and the courage it has taken to open myself back up to it. I deserve, in short, to honor and relish my personal journey deeper into self and deeper into my relationship with Eros. Pleasure magic is about relearning that simple fact and honoring the sorrows that get unearthed as you reclaim your divine right to happiness.

Pleasure is an Integral Part of Everyday Life.
So often what we think of when we think of pleasure is highly extroverted and performative, as with most things mainstream culture celebrates. (See a pattern here with things that "should" feel right but are actually kind of draining?) Pleasure gets relegated to a wild Saturday night out or a fabulous birthday bash. That's too stingy! Pleasure should be—and is—part of our everyday life. We just have to slow down and allow ourselves to experience it.

I'm pretty routine-driven—or, should I say, *ritual*-driven. You'd think I'd get bored after a while, but the truth is, I relish the simple weekly events as they unfold, from returning to work on Monday, cleaning my house on Wednesday, and going to the grocery store on Thursday. That's saying nothing of the smaller simple pleasures like brewing a cup of chamomile tea before I go to bed or getting a few more rows in the blanket I'm knitting. Each one is a concrete manifestation of the joyful life I'm conjuring for myself.

Simple Pleasures are Sacred—and thus, to be Protected.
It is so easy to numb out in our day-to-day life, particularly when we're moving too fast or feeling over-worked. We begin to skate over the little things that bring us joy, like that morning cup of coffee or the later afternoon walk. Even as we do those things, knowing full well how much we look forward to them each day, our minds are elsewhere. Have you ever eaten a meal home with no memory of how the dish tasted? It's kind of like

that. We move on autopilot and, as a result, deprive ourselves of those soulful daily delights that make life delicious. We get too serious—*I don't have time for that!*—and downplay our need for happiness, playfulness.

It's such an easy thing to get trapped in, particularly because it is so socially acceptable to be overworked and depleted. Which is why I've learned to take some of the energy I put into working hard and use it to protect my simple pleasures. I treat them as sacred. I privilege them in the same way I used to privilege getting work done and taking care of others. They are equally important, one not outweighing the other.

I also realized that part of my ability to experience pleasure relies on a sense of safety. If I'm in a place or situation that doesn't make me feel comfortable, I can't relax enough to enjoy myself. If I'm overworked or around people that make me anxious, my capacity for feeling good things diminishes. So, I protect my energy, getting rid of anything that gets in the way of the sacredness of experiencing simple pleasures, anything that doesn't make me feel safe. As a result, I enjoy a more balanced life that is all the sweeter for the time I take time to stop and smell the roses.

Questions to ask yourself:

What pleasure do you allow yourself to enjoy?
What do you need to do to feel safe opening yourself to pleasure?
How can you create space for sacred simple pleasures?

Routine as Ritual: Welcoming Sacred Simple Pleasures into Your Everyday

Rest . . . Without Guilt.
Get a full night's rest every night. Take naps. Spend an afternoon reading or otherwise losing track of time. I know this feels like

a tough one, when it feels like finishing everything on the day's to-do list is more important, or unplugging enough to take that nap can feel like its own challenge, but as with all magic, it is so worth it! I invoke the power of my familiar here. My black cat is shameless in his pursuit of naps, relaxation, and downtime. He reminds me when I am tempted to keep working or feeling guilty (it's a hard thing to unlearn) that rest and relaxation are key to a magical life. Everything on my list all gets done eventually anyway, and I'm a better person for time away from my desk. I'm also realizing that my ability to take a nap, for example, is a great way to gauge my work-life balance. If I can't power down for a little cat nap, I'm too wired. If I can, I know I've achieved that right balance of enjoying the simple pleasure of a job well done and the simple pleasure of restoration.

Prioritize Sacred Simple Pleasures Throughout the Day.
I'm in the process of outgrowing a habit where I sit at my writing desk first thing in the morning, coffee cup in hand…and go down the rabbit hole of answering emails, then prepping for a day of writing and teaching. Before I know it, a few hours have gone by, and I still haven't eaten breakfast! Now I'm working on enjoying a cup of coffee on my patio or an early morning walk, then a tasty breakfast, before turning to my desk. My workday is all the more pleasurable for the time I take to enjoy my morning rituals. I prioritize work breaks throughout the day—a mid-morning cup of tea, a short walk, listening to a podcast or audiobook. The kicker? I get just as much done as I did when I focused solely on my job. But now, I'm more refreshed and end the day on a lighter note. Then there are other things I pepper throughout my day, like Latin dance. I don't always want to be at a crowded bar dancing the night away, but I'm not above shaking it at home to my favorite salsa songs while washing dishes. That's the beauty of sacred simple pleasures: they don't have to be elaborate. Sometimes, they are as sweet and spicy as dancing the cha-cha

in your pajamas while making soup.

Tune in to What You're Feeling.
This one might seem kind of strange, but in all honesty, sometimes enjoying yourself—experiencing an overwhelming emotion—opens up the floodgates for you to feel other things that you might have buried or haven't been receptive or ready to feel just yet. Not all of them are pleasant. But they all have their purpose. Mending our relationship to pleasure allows us to safely process difficult emotions and heal old wounds. Think of opening yourself to pleasure as going from living in black and white to technicolor. Your senses are heightened. The world is a kaleidoscope of energies you've never seen before. I admit this can sometimes be a bittersweet pleasure. The key to keeping this a healthy experience is to feel what you need to feel...and then let it go. When something comes up for me during the day, I take a moment to check in with myself and explore what this feeling, however uncomfortable, is telling me. It's a good idea to think about what caused a certain emotion to surface. Acknowledge it. Take in the wisdom. Then move on. Restore yourself by enjoying one of your sacred simple pleasures.

Conjuring Everyday Magic: Opening Up to Eros Energy

Fill Your Home with Things that Give You Joy.
I'll be honest. I'm old enough to know what I like and what I don't, which means I've given up the idea of keeping things around my home to make other people happy. If something creeps me out, makes me sad, or simply doesn't make me smile when I see it—even if it was a gift—then it doesn't belong in my home. *I deserve to be surrounded by things that make me happy.* That's the spell I repeat to myself whenever I have to let go of something that compromises the vibe in my sanctuary. Our homes are an expression of ourselves and our most intimate

spaces. It only makes sense that we fill that space with things that inspire, soothe, or otherwise delight us.

In fact, one of my favorite sacred simple pleasures is curating my home to invite in the divine hedonism of Eros. I love adding new art to the spaces on my walls that feel bare and rearranging my bookshelf in all its joyful chaos (again, I only fill it with books that nourish and inspire). I hang dried garlic bulbs in my kitchen and organize the goods in my pantry in various jars and glass containers to inspire impromptu kitchen witchery. I cover my nightstand with crystals and paperbacks so that I wake up to beautiful objects first thing in the morning. If my energy feels stagnant, I move furniture around or fluff pillows to give myself a new perspective on life. Take a look around your own home. Does everything welcome in Eros energy?

Wear Only Things that Make You Feel Beautiful.
I have this shirt—it's oversized and sage green, with a whimsical tree printed on it, with wild branches and sturdy roots, that praises the wonders of composting. I just feel so beautiful every time I wear it. It isn't fancy. It isn't what you would call sexy. But I love it. I feel like an earth goddess every time I put it on. I'm reminded of the beautiful life I create every time I turn my compost and water my plants with compost tea. Then there are my dresses—many of them vintage-inspired—that make me feel just lovely. I've given up wearing things that make me feel bad about myself. You know the clothes. The *When I Lose Weight* clothes and the *Maybe I Can Make This Style Work* clothes. Or worse, the *This Was a Gift So I Have to Wear It* clothes. At the end of the day, what you wear is not only a form of armor as you make your way in the world, but a celebration of your spirit. How can you feel like the human incarnation of Eros or Aphrodite when what you're wearing makes you feel bad about yourself? Wear what brings you joy. Period.

Read Romance Novels.

Seriously! My love affair with romance novels was one of those slow-burn affairs that started when I was in college, a brown woman looking for stories about happy endings. Those are hard things to come by when you're underrepresented and almost all the stories about you in history and in media are about oppression and injustice. So, I found a home in 18th- and 19th-Century British romance novels. They always had happy endings. And they featured women like me—women in search of soul, purpose, and joy in a world that didn't always make space for them. Granted, my skin was darker than the heroines of those novels, and those stories never addressed the culturally specific issues I had to work with to develop and maintain my own HEA, but they taught me a great deal about what it meant to find my own joy.

Then came the modern romance novel. This is a hot and heavy affair that has no end in sight. I found these books at a time when I was most in need of reclaiming my capacity for pleasure. I read so many books about women of color and other minorities having their own HEAs. They didn't have to choose between the dream job and the dream partner. Their identity and growth weren't always centered on their minority status. They had their own agency and autonomy, their own power to choose and craft a fulfilling life. Plus, passionate consensual sex! These books are Eros energy incarnate, all about healthy, joyful relationality with oneself and others. Reading these books filled me with joy and helped me reconnect to the simple pleasure of reading and dreaming. If romance novels aren't your thing (but don't knock them 'til you try them!), read whatever will help you relax and enjoy the sacred simple pleasure of a good book.

Chapter 5

Be Open to Synchronicity

Okay, so you're nice and loose from all the pleasure magic you've been doing. Now it's time to open yourself to the unseen world and the subtle magic of signs and coincidences. If radical self-care is about tuning in to your own needs and nourishing your internal life, then synchronicity is tuning in to an ongoing conversation with the Universe. Synchronicity, defined as a meaningful coincidence, is the act of looking for signs from the Universe. Hokey as it might sound, it is real. You just have to be willing to listen and open your eyes to the unseen world. These meaningful signs pepper our lives, and offer valuable insights and messages from the Universe if we are willing to listen. Some of my most powerful revelations have come out of seemingly innocuous moments that served to punctuate an important feeling, experience, or situation. Like a bolt of lightning, it serves to illuminate the magic in your life and remind you that there is more to life than what the surface shows.

Still, a synchronous event is a hard thing to describe, mostly because it is so personal. What I can say is that you'll know when you see it. Rather, you'll know it when you *feel* it. Synchronicity, at its heart, is about the interconnectedness of all things. We are the Universe, and the Universe is us. These signs are deeply tied to our own experiences and psyches, so what might be a life-changing mystic message for one person is meaningless to another. It's its own secret love language between you and the Universe. For example, I tend to get a lot of animal wisdom in the form of roadrunners and ladybugs. That's because the roadrunner is a powerful symbol for repelling evil in the desert Southwest (it's also the state bird of New Mexico). Their crossed claws create tracks that make it difficult to tell which direction they are moving in, a trait that is said to confuse and dispel evil. As for the ladybugs, well, I just happen to really love ladybugs! It's like I'm already attuned to their magic, so whenever they cross my path, I'm able to see them and take in the wisdom they offer. I'm also drawn to flipping through books and dealing tarot as more concrete ways of asking questions and finding synchronous answers.

But synchronicity comes in other forms too, and not always in the way we expect it or prefer it. That's its power—it works in a random confluence of events that somehow resonates with our personal psyches. How did I know to trust my instincts that a relationship was well and truly over? I was thinking about the whole situation and, when I turned on my car, the radio blasted, "the thrill is gone..." Boy, was it, and to ignore that would only cause more heartache. And what gave me the courage to turn my blog posts into the manuscript that would become my award-winning book *Everyday Enchantments*? A random folded paper tucked into an old paperback I'd decided to reread. On that piece of paper was a series of scribbles from my teenage self, thinking about the day when I would be An Adult and a Published Author. I started working on my new manuscript that afternoon.

Several years ago, I considered taking a job that didn't quite work with my personal values and professional goals just to expand my resume. I was driving while mulling my options over and considering the job. I wound up taking a wrong turn and found myself staring at a literal dead end. That's when I knew that job wasn't for me. Or take the uncanny feeling I had when walking into a space for the first time and recognizing everything, from the sparkling lighting to the retro decor. It turns out, I had been to that space before; I'd literally dreamed about it the previous night. Guess I was in the right place.

Deciding to blog on everyday magic—what seems like ages ago—was a big decision. I came from a more conservative academic writing background that made me question every creative impulse. Yet, as I contemplated blogging, I was confronted by positive affirmations that banished the self-doubt that inevitably crept up. Roadrunners, those perennial good-luck signs, crossed my path at unexpected times. I stumbled across a nest of ladybugs, those cheerful creatures, and walked into a flurry of floating dandelion puffs, like so many wishes cast to the sky. There was even the random kind message from a friend, letting me know they appreciated my world view. There it was. Life was telling me to move forward with this venture. I'm glad I listened to those signs, because it was the start of my writing career.

One week, a hawk crossed my path. The bird swooped down and rested on a recycling bin outside a nearby house. That came at the end of a day in which I'd been wrestling with my intuition, which seemed to be telling me something counter to what I felt I should be doing. I'd been trying to talk myself into taking on more work than was reasonable, because the thought of saying no, of disappointing someone, was a weight that felt too heavy to carry. But my gut reaction at the request was to turn it down, as I'd already taken on too many extra projects in the past and was just then getting to a place where I could breathe again. The hawk reminded me to trust my intuition and get some perspective—a *bird's-eye view* of my situation. It also asked me to be ferocious, like the hawk, in protecting my territory, or in my case, my boundaries. It helped. I stopped worrying it over in my mind and let it rest. I let myself feel how I needed to feel and gave myself some much-needed quiet time. Then the answers came.

The skeptic might think these examples are just random events to which I've decided to apply meaning. To which I say, *you need more magic in your life!* Anyone who has been touched by the power of synchronicity knows it's real. And yes, to a certain extent, I am applying meaning to random events—that's what synchronicity is. But there's an electric energy to synchronicity, which I once literally tapped into when I was talking about pursuing a more traditional academic scholarly career.

I was at the start of my career and trying to figure out what would be the best (read: most fulfilling) path for me to take. The electricity literally sparked out as I was talking about a more conventional academic path. I guessed that was a road I shouldn't go down, which turned out to be true. Instead of pursuing a tenure-track career, which would keep me from New Mexico and limit my ability to prioritize student success in diverse communities, I focused my career development on working in inclusive, student-centered colleges. The freedom that opened up from this choice also allowed me to pursue the kind of writing I wanted to—non-fiction and fiction that spoke to a broader range of people, not just academics.

Here's another synchronous moment. I've always been interested in tarot. I'd lately been thinking that it was time to get a deck. It was a thought that kept coming back and one that I didn't mention to anyone. Then, for my birthday later that week, I received my first tarot deck from my parents. They said they'd read about it and it made them think of me—it was a feeling that wouldn't go away. Clearly, the Universe was telling me that studying tarot was a good idea and was making sure I started on the right foot. My first deck was the Motherpeace tarot, which centers women and people of color in its iconography. It remains my favorite deck because it decenters patriarchy and whiteness with rounded cards that explore the Divine Feminine. This put me on the path to studying tarot more seriously, including completing several creative projects guided by its wisdom.

Without those insights—those little nudges from life telling me I was on the right track or ready to move on—I wouldn't have been brave enough to listen to my inner wisdom. You would be surprised what the Universe is willing to reveal if you simply ask it and stay open to the answers it might give. The rush of insight, the disorientation of being connected to something beyond the ordinary—those are real feelings. Trust them. Nurture them. Look for them and they will speak. Then you listen and follow through with its message. It will always guide you back to your inner magic.

Invite Synchronicity into Your Life

Interestingly, synchronicity is less about relearning and unlearning life lessons like the other foundational elements of everyday magic. You've already done so much of that work, which has now left you receptive to the hidden messages of the unseen world. The primary task of exploring the world of meaningful coincidence is to take all you've learned in your previous magical practices and use it to open yourself up to a world of intuitive possibility. You have to welcome this energy into your life in the same way you did Goddess energy and Eros energy, everyday magic and self-care. It's what you used to transform your routines into rituals and the ordinary into enchanted moments. In essence, this is where you can let your full witchy self shine and celebrate your connection to the Universe. Here's are a few tips for how to get started.

Get Loose.
Real talk: we live in a world that values concrete, rational things. These are all good and well in their right place, but synchronicity is a different kind of literacy all together. It's about opening yourself to the possibility of a new way of being. Often times, our innate instincts and unfiltered feelings get buried under the pressure to conform to social norms. Instead of allowing ourselves to introvert when we need to introvert, for example, we push past our needs and do more, get louder, and move faster despite our soul's longing for quiet. Loosening up allows us to let go of rigid expectations or assumptions about how things should be so we can be open to the magic around us.

Get Playful.

When was the last time you stayed up past your bedtime reading? Or ditched the to-do list in favor of a schedule-free Saturday? Or danced in your pajamas to your favorite song? If it has been a while, now is the time to welcome that playful energy into your life. Be like the otter, an animal that devotes as much time to play as it does to work. Why? I'll let you in on a little secret: Synchronicity is pretty darn playful. It's a lot like Coyote, the archetypal trickster, sneaking up on you when you least expect it, catching you off guard, forcing you to rethink your world view. The best way to be open to these insights is to let go of hard and fast rules and just get playful.

Get Curious.

Synchronicity is all about opening yourself up to the world and remembering that child-like curiosity about new places and things that delights the senses. This kind of energy loves questions, exploration, expansion. Often our sense of wonder gets lost as we succumb to the demands of our day-in, day-out life. Take a moment—pause, breathe deeply, and think about what it used to feel like when the changing seasons created a sense of unblemished excitement for something new, or the way a sunset was like an open invitation to marvel at the beauty of life, or how a winding dirt road was the promise of an adventure. Then turn that innate curiosity on your inner landscape—forget to push and prod and contain difficult feelings or old selves, and simply marvel at the fact that you contain multitudes, like so many tiny cosmic seeds waiting to be explored. Synchronicity is found in these silent, joyful explorations.

How to Listen to the Messages

Sometimes we throw out questions to the Universe and get an answer instantly, maybe a week or month from then. More often than not, however, the answers come when we've forgotten to fixate on whatever it is we want answers to. Sometimes we even get nudges and insights to things we didn't know we even had questions about. Or signs jump out at us to make us pay attention to the unseen world when our vision gets a little too *mundane*— something that can easily happen when you are in a world that is uncomfortable with brown woman magic or otherness in any form. You can start to regulate yourself. You can start to shut down. When that happens (unlearning is an ongoing exercise), return to the chapter on pleasure magic. It should help you shake whatever rigidity is setting in.

Synchronicity is like that, trickster that it is, deciding what questions you get answers to and which ones you just have to struggle with on your own. It's a lot like tarot, I Ching, or other forms of divination. Asking when in need will offer valuable insights to guide you. Using it too often and becoming dependent on reading the cards leads to muddy answers. They literally shut down because they don't want you overly dependent on them at the cost of your own inner voice. That way leads to disempowerment and, in its own way, getting rigid about one way of seeing the world. Likewise, don't be flip about your questions or treat divination, including synchronicity, like a party trick. That's a good way to piss off those energies. You don't want to be on the wrong side of those comic vibes.

So instead, allow your energy to flow, be flexible, and let answers to your deepest questions come to you in their own way, in their own time. And remember that sometimes, no answer is an answer. It's kind of like the Universe saying that whatever it is you are worried about is a non-issue. Or if it sees you forgetting to enjoy the wonder around you, well, like Coyote, it won't hesitate to shake up your order a bit. Synchronicity comes into your life as a reminder to tune into the magic of your every day. Often the wisdom it imparts is immediately and intuitively understood, so don't worry it like you would a loose thread on your jacket. Just feel what it is asking you to feel. The answers will come.

The more you invite synchronicity into your life, the more it will manifest unbidden. It only ever needs your time and attention to reveal itself to you wholeheartedly and without restraint. And with more meaningful, soul-illuminating coincidences comes more magic.

Questions to ask yourself:

> *What images, animals, and symbols regularly speak to me?*
> *When am I most connected to the Universe and its messages?*
> *What actions and behaviors make me more receptive to the synchronous?*

Routine as Ritual: Making Synchronicity Part of Your Everyday

Explore the Tarot.

Sometimes the idea of opening up to meaningful coincidences can feel too unstructured or open-ended when you're starting out. Tarot cards are a great place to begin your journey into the world of synchronicity because they are a little more contained. You're asking your questions and, by a random shuffling of the deck, you're getting your answers. There are many different ways to use the cards, and even more ways to arrange them in meaningful reading patterns. For me, simple is always better. I like to think of a question, or sometimes just a feeling or situation I've been pondering, while I hold the cards. When it feels right, I pull a card from the deck. I then read up on it to learn what insights it can offer to my current situation. If I need a little more guidance, I draw three cards for past, present, and future. They tell me where I've been, where I am, and where I'm going in relation to my chosen question. Too many cards (at least for me) and the meaning begins to feel muddled. The goal here, especially in terms of synchronicity, is to stay loose, which means looking at the big picture and immediate impressions that the cards reveal.

Look to Books.

I have always been a big proponent of book magic. Before I embraced my bruja lifestyle, they were the things I regularly went to for answers. The stories they tell us and the things we read at the right time in our lives (more synchronicity at work) nourish us when nothing else can. They can also be useful tools for guidance when you need a little extra insight.

Here's how to do it: Go to your bookshelf and choose a book that is calling to you. It doesn't have to be something witchy or divination-based. I've found as much wisdom in a sword and sorcery paperback or romance as I have in a foundational psychology or spirituality text. What matters is that you choose a book that's calling to you, even if you've never read it before (who doesn't have a ton of unread books on their shelves?). Hold the book in your hand and think about your question or situation, or simply be present in the thoughts and feelings running through you. When it feels like it's time, flip through the book without looking. Again, when it feels right, open up to a page. You can place a finger randomly on that page or simply let your eyes fall where they will. Read the passage you've found. What insight does it offer? Be warned, though. This is one of the divination tools that only works sporadically. If you do this too much, the books stop speaking via synchronicity.

Ask for a Sign.

Sometimes we need to remember that we are magic. Take the black cat that crossed my path every few days for a week in my office parking lot. It was sleek and well-groomed, but without a collar. It didn't look like a stray. In fact, it looked exactly like it knew where it was going. It would simply strut in front of my car along the little dirt path by the ditch that separated my campus from the neighborhood park. It didn't rush. It didn't sneak from car to car. It just *was*.

Every time I saw that cat, I felt bold and magical and fully *bruja*. It occurred to me the third time I saw that magical black cat that I'd been asking for a sign. I was feeling burned out. Burdened by bureaucracy. Unable to feel my inner magic. I was looking for a sign that would tell me my decision to pull back on my workload was a wise one, because guilt, that perpetual energetic drain, was making me feel bad for wanting more work-life balance. Then the black cat came. Unconcerned by what anyone thought about it and simply going its own way. There was my sign to keep moving in my new direction. It was important, too, that it happened at work. I was allowed to return to my quiet magic, walk my own path. Sometimes, inviting synchronicity into your life is as simple as asking for a sign.

Everyday Conjuring: Inviting Synchronicity into Your Life

Practice Free Association.
This is all part of learning to stay loose. When we get too tight, too literal, our magic dries up. When we get loose, we're able to do things like free-associate. This is not to be confused with trivializing our relationship to the synchronous—a dangerous thing to do—rather, it's about honoring the power of spontaneity. Free association is about letting your mind focus on whatever random idea, memory or impression it happens to land on. It's a way of sinking into the unconscious mind to better understand yourself and your needs. Basically, you bypass what your conscious mind perceives to be important so that you can see what is really significant through uncensored exploration. When you get used to listening to your psyche, looking for signs becomes a more fluid practice.

Tune into What You're Feeling.
This is right in line with your pleasure magic practice. Especially if you are a minority, it can be hard to open yourself to these things because we are so conditioned not to be vulnerable in order to survive. So, we push things down or bottle things up. We get busy so we don't have to deal with the emotions that will bubble to the surface if we let ourselves be still. All that does, however, is block our energy, disconnecting us from ourselves and the Universe. Opening yourself to the world of synchronicity is, in part, about cultivating a greater sensitivity to self. Make sure to check in with yourself throughout the day, particularly if you start to feel like you're moving too fast, you've become disconnected from your routine, or a particular situation causes unexpected feelings to flare up. This form of emotional literacy will help you better interpret the synchronous events in your life as your emotional life and the secret world of signs are deeply connected.

Look for Wisdom in the Ordinary.
Avoid looking for big neon lightning-bolt signs. Look instead for the little things that offer profound meaning for you. They might seem innocuous, but their wisdom will indeed feel like a lightning bolt. Pay attention to what you see in any given moment and think about what it means. Or rather, think about how it makes you feel. What is the hidden message there? And remember, stay loose! Often your first impression is the right one.

Take the time I was getting too wound up and wrapped up in worries. I went for a walk to clear out, and my eyes lit on a beautiful little ladybug resting on a nearby bush. When I got closer to inspect it, I noticed that the ladybug was actually stuck in a spider's web. The symbolism hit me hard—my joy was trapped by stressful thoughts of things I couldn't control. I had to free myself from that sticky web if I wanted my natural ease to return. I freed the ladybug—it happily crawled along my fingers for a little bit until it flew off in search of safer territories. I thanked it for its message and reminded myself to beware spidery traps of my own making. Now, that little scene might not have meant something to someone else, but for me, with my love of ladybugs, it was a pure act of synchronicity.

Chapter 6

Live Beyond the Expected

Here we are. Almost at the end of the road. In fact, here's where we can joyfully get off the road and chart a new path. We've spent the last few chapters learning how to decondition ourselves, unlearning harmful, internalized social constructs, and relearning our infinite capacity for joy. Now we get to create space for the unexpected. Or, better put, live beyond the expected. You'll notice that this chapter won't be quite as *structured* as the others, and that's the point! We get to loosen the reins a little. Explore everyday magic now that we've comfortably established our day-in, day-out conjurings.

This is perhaps the most ephemeral and delicious part of cultivating everyday magic. It is also one of the most difficult aspects of embracing your inner witch, because it is more passive work. It's about being open, receptive to the gentle pull of your heart's desire and the synchronous events that call to you. The amorphousness of it can feel disconcerting at first, especially if you have a lot of action-oriented fire energy like me. The temptation to chart your spiritual growth by concrete accomplishments rather than something as incorporeal as energetic expansiveness is strong. But the danger in relying solely on the tangible is that we can limit our expansiveness and our potential. We fill up every corner of our mind with facts and deadlines, leaving little room for the imagination to conjure up something delightfully unexpected. And it's understandable. The unknown is terrifying.

What if we create space and all we get is a void? What if nothing happens? Hey, nobody said magic wasn't scary. It takes a lot of belief and a heaping helping of hope to trust that the Universe has your back when you stop shackling yourself to busy, fast, checklist living. The thing is, you have to be willing to pay the price for that kind of magic—to let go of things you hold on to because they are familiar and comforting, but not all that helpful or healthy. It's like the old fairytales where the heroine has to see past the glamour and illusion of society in order to see the mystic world beyond it. Only, in this fairytale, you're seeing beyond the ordinary into a world of magic—if you're willing to let go of the things mainstream culture values.

Living beyond the expected is all about invoking Divine Receptivity. Think of those lazy summer afternoons when your biggest concern was daydreaming, the deep dreams that whisk you away into other worlds and dimensions, reminding you that you are more than just one demand after another; that you are allowed to reach—want—more than a life full of paperwork. Between your new daily rituals, commitment to radical self-care, and pleasure magic practice, you've got the solid foundation for conjuring this deeply feminine receptive energy—this luscious Goddess energy.

The best way to explain this Divine Receptivity is to tell you a story about the time I'd worn myself out by overwork and extreme extroversion. Who hasn't succumbed to the demands of a world that wants more, louder, and faster? I'd worked hard through my twenties to pay my way through graduate school and establish myself in my teaching and writing careers. My thirties hit and I had one of those mini life crises worthy of a romantic comedy. I began to wonder if I'd missed out on all the partying and finding-yourself exploration stuff that the media represents as what people do in their twenties. So, I made a point of doing all the things I thought could be fun, or should be fun, to see if I had, indeed, missed out.

Turns out, I hadn't missed a thing. Sure, I had some fun experiences and felt a growing confidence in the realization that hanging out with people was no big deal (when you're an introvert and career focused, people can sometimes make you feel like you're a social invalid, incapable of common social interactions). I even discovered things I continue to enjoy and participate in. But what I remember most was how tired and anxious I was during that time. I'd finish a long work week and then pump myself up for more people, activities, events. On the rare occasion I didn't have anything planned or a friend had to cancel, I was secretly relieved. I could stay home! In my jammies! And watch a silly movie and be in bed by 8:30! It was bliss.

That quiet, homey time made me realize that in my attempt to figure myself out, I'd actually *worn* myself out. Even worse, I realized that a serious motivation behind these explorations was an attempt to feel more normal or socially acceptable. I worked super hard to establish myself in my profession, battling issues of impostor syndrome and presumed incompetence by day, and then went out at night to prove I was a well-rounded person. The thing was, it didn't actually make me happy. I was glad for the experiment—part of everyday magic is learning what you don't want—but I was even happier to see the end of it.

But when it came time to pull back on my extreme extroversion, I hesitated. Sure, I was eager to nourish my introverted heart and devote more time to exploring what work-life balance and enjoyment looked like for me out side of the more performative aspects I'd been caught up in. Yet, another part of me was afraid. I was shocked by this revelation, which came to me after a healing yoga practice. What if I pulled back and there was nothing there? What if my life was empty? What if I was giving up important things that I could never get back? Panic surged in me.

I paused to examine those feelings. I knew I wasn't happy being as extroverted as I was acting, and yet I worried that I wouldn't be able to find my own path. That somehow mainstream culture was right, I was wrong, and I need to try harder to fit into this unrealistic mold of being a successful (brown) woman who has it all. That was the heart of it. What if I pulled back, allowed myself to imagine a different kind of life, and nothing ever came of it? It was a risk worth taking, I decided.

So, I let go of things that were slowly making me feel pressured. I dropped for-fun classes that stopped being fun as I was increasingly asked to take extracurricular things more seriously than I wanted to. I turned down social plans when I felt too tired to go out, and I resisted the temptation to say yes to every new work project. *I did enough. I was enough.* I had to remind myself of both those things frequently. Having it all was impossible—nobody could, or should, have it all. I was learning how to curate a life filled with things I enjoyed rather than feeling like I needed to do everything for fear of missing out.

I also had to closely examine where that pressure to do more was coming from. As an introvert and woman of color, I found that so much of the pressure I felt to be a visibly active part of all my communities was coming from that sense of *less-than*. Unconsciously, I felt like it was my job to make myself unconditionally available to others at work and in my social life. It was rare that I asked myself what I wanted. What work projects were most in alignment with my pedagogy and values? What social interactions nourished me? Was I excited about that date or did I feel obligated to show the world I was actively looking for The One? This, I've learned, is not an uncommon experience, especially for women of color. When you are an othered body, you are often asked to take on the labor—emotional, social, literal—of those who see you as a commodity, consciously or unconsciously. Worse, I'd internalized and reinforced those toxic norms with my own behavior. That's why I had been tired and anxious all the time. It was time to take my power back.

As it turns out, the process of finding yourself is in the everyday—just like magic. Not in the fear-of-missing-out frenzy. Not in the performative adventures. But in the day-in, day-out process of living, working, relating, dreaming with intention. When we acknowledge that simple truth, we reclaim our personal power and the right to live deeply as we choose.

All my extroverted actions were fundamentally about proving my worth and trying to have it all. So many narratives about women, particularly professionally successful women of color like myself, are narratives about having to choose between career and relationships. Between working hard and living life. It is rare that you are allowed to be seen as someone who can be both professionally successful and personally fulfilled. You are taught that you can't ask for too much, so you have to choose one or the other. Inevitably, you become a self-fulfilling prophecy—you visibly excel in one area and feel the deficit in another—unless you actively and consciously work through the limits people place on your joy and how you've internalized those restrictions.

When I took a step back, I realized that part of why I was feeling burned out was because I'd gotten too caught up in what other people were telling me about my life. How it should look. What I should be doing. How I should feel about it. Then I got all wound up and anxious about everything. It wasn't until I made the conscious choice to think about what I wanted, not what other people expected of me, that I was able to find my way. Granted, the end of this journey coincided with the pandemic, which literally enforced my need for space as we followed stay-at-home orders in New Mexico. The shocking reality of that time, however, was that I didn't miss much, if anything, of my social life prior to this slower, less social way of life. The things I had loved beforehand carried on in other forms, usually online. Those I didn't, faded away.

I got rid of mindless busy and created space for life to happen. It was hard at first to trust that I was doing the right thing. The space felt empty and cavernous, and I constantly had to stop myself from filling it because that was what I was used to doing. It's an ongoing process, to be sure. But I keep at it because of one magic truth: when I created space for the unexpected, things started happening.

The biggest shift was that I began to feel better. I had my quiet time to replenish myself and so enjoyed people more when I did go out, pre-pandemic. I felt my creative energy blossom as new inspiration for books, blogs, and other writing projects bubbled out of me. A day didn't go by without some synchronous event or another happening, guiding me to new adventures and profound insights. I met people who understood and valued me as I was, not who I thought I should be. I healed my relationship with myself. I tapped into the divine wisdom of nature, allowed myself to move beyond limiting social structures that asked me to hide my magic for a world that doesn't always want to believe in it.

I realized that I had placed limits on my potential. Creating space for life to unfold allowed me to become more expansive, more playful, more hopeful. I was no longer trapped by the life I thought I should be living. Kind of a long story, but what it boils down to is this: If you want to experience everyday magic, you need to create space for it to speak to you. You can't see it or feel it if you're moving too fast or are disconnected from yourself. Magic only reveals itself to those willing to pause, listen, and be open to wonder.

Here's how.

Conjuring the Delightfully Unexpected

Create Space.
Literally! Let go of anything and everything in your home that no longer serves you. Truth be told, my home will never be fashionably minimalist—it's more like a hobbit hole, filled with things that make me happy and bring me comfort. But there's plenty of space. I feel like I can breathe there. Everything in my sanctuary has a purpose and beauty. I avoid buying anything just to buy it, and make sure that I enjoy everything I have. If things are too cluttered, I clean, I reorganize, I let stuff go. Do

the same thing to your office, your online life, your mind, and all the other important spaces you inhabit. Holding on to too much stuff leads to stagnant energy, as well as an invitation to ghosts to manifest themselves in the objects you've outgrown but are afraid to let go of.

Make Time.

Clear your calendar. Ruthlessly. This has been a tough one for me. Sometimes, I cut back on work only to fill up my downtime with more things to do. I start the work week tired because, as fun as all the things I did seemed, they also wore me out. I'm beginning to think of too much structured time as inherently unhealthy for energetic flow. Don't get me wrong—I love a full, robust life. Just not one without plenty of time to rest and relax. This is something I'm still working on, and no doubt will be for the rest of my life. That's because part of what I'm working through are issues of impostor syndrome and presumed incompetence. It can be a toxic cycle—you overwork to prove your worth, and fear cutting back because it might make you look lazy, so you keep working. That's where brujería comes in. With it, I remind myself that I am allowed to be empowered, expansive, and yes, sometimes hedonistically unproductive. In fact, I think that last part is essential to conjuring everyday magic.

Unstructured time is key to being receptive to living beyond the tightly conventional life we are often expected to live. When we pave the way for synchronicity and the unexpected, we offer ourselves the opportunity to live a life we haven't yet had the imagination to dream up. The next step is freeing your mind. Relearn what it means to let your mind wander. To daydream. If you find yourself fixating on a negative situation or attempting to anticipate every bad thing that might happen, ask yourself why. It seems like an awful waste of an imagination. Spend a little time with the problem to explore a solution or your feelings about it, and then let it go. We are conditioned to fixate on the negative so much so that we have to relearn what it means to nourish the life-affirming.

Free Your Mind.

We keep a lot of mental clutter. We might have let go of the tangible objects holding us back or removed ourselves from spaces that make us feel constrained, but freeing our mind from returning to those things? That's a whole other issue. We're conditioned to focus on the negative—the problem, the issue that has defined us for so long. Sometimes it's harder to dream up a solution or imagine another way of living. It takes conscious effort not to recreate the problems you left in your head. It's essential to leave them, but there's also a comfort in knowing what those things are, so it's tempting to hang onto them. Don't. Every time you find your mind wandering to rehash old conversations or conjure up would-be problems, stop. Let them go. Then spend some time nourishing your fantasy life. Seriously! Take all the energy you've spent on problems and turn it toward delicious potentials.

Let Go of Expectations.

Think of living beyond the expected as unlearning social norms that prefer you be *less-than*, and so, easier to contain and manage. You are literally detoxing. There will be inevitable ups and downs to that process. Days when you feel the full power of your freedom and other days when you wonder why you got off the main path in the first place. What matters is that you give yourself the time and space to work through the emotions that come up as you're exploring your inner world. This also means letting go of a clear agenda or idea of what progress should look like. This is not a linear path, more like an unplanned saunter where your direction is decided by how you feel at each fork in the road. Trust your instincts here and enjoy the playful energy of zero expectations. Make the only thing on your agenda trusting your healing process, in whatever form that takes for the day. Realign yourself with the flow of life and resist the pressure to have a clear plan.

Questions to ask yourself:

What am I holding on to out of fear?
What am I afraid to embrace?
What is the most delicious life I can conjure for myself?

Living Beyond the Expected

This next part will feel a little like a waiting game for those of us used to being more action-oriented. It's also one of the more difficult aspects of everyday magic to describe. Like powerful synchronous experiences, living beyond the expected is something that looks different for everyone, something you'll instinctively know when you feel it. And like synchronicity, sometimes the best way to describe a more magical way of life is through storytelling.

Now seems like a good time to tell you the story about how I met my familiar, Smoke. I was at a crossroads and in desperate need of a sign that told me that magic was real. That I was on the right path. It was in the middle of a difficult year of letting go of things that no longer served me, coming to terms with who I am — an introvert, someone who was burned out on over-work and too much busy. I'd drawn boundaries and let go of things. I was, in short, in the midst of making room for the unexpected. It was a hard, painful process that left me depleted and wondering if there was a purpose to so much pain. Self-doubt set in. Who was I to buck social convention? What was I thinking? These were small, quiet thoughts I hadn't even acknowledged to myself. Without consciously thinking it, I was looking for a sign from the Universe, a reminder that everyday magic is real and that I was on the right path.

So, I went to one of the places I knew would reconnect me to magic: my local bookstore. I had a feeling that surrounding myself with stories, so many paperback possibilities, would be enough to revive my senses. Here's the thing: I didn't end up buying a single book that day. But I did meet my familiar.

I walked into the bookstore, where they were hosting cat adoptions, and saw the cutest little black kitten. It was love at first sight! I tried to keep a firm head on my shoulders, however, and think about all the practical issues of cat ownership. I'd never had a cat and, in fact, had purposely never gotten a pet for very logical reasons. I lived in an apartment, which wouldn't be fair to dogs, who need space to run around. I had been working long hours, which is also not fair to any animal waiting for me to come home. I was also aggressively paying off debt, so I didn't want to add any extra expenses at the moment. But none of that mattered when I saw that nine-month-old shadow.

By the time I had him in my arms—where he comfortably settled without clawing or biting—I knew I was a goner. We were fast friends. Suddenly I couldn't imagine my life without this little familiar. Still, in an attempt to be responsible, I did spend some time googling cat care to make sure there wasn't anything that would scare me away. Nothing did. I knew we'd figure things out together. By evening, I was back at my apartment with my new cat, Smoke (named after the occult detective, John Silence's cat, who accompanies him on his paranormal investigations—but that's another story for another time), armed with lots of advice from the cat-loving bookstore ladies and a hastily purchased arsenal of feline necessities.

In the space of a few hours, I'd gone from doubting myself and my choice to live a slower, quieter—and more magical—life, to being swept off my feet by an iconically witchy black cat. Talk about the unexpected! None of the concerns I might usually have had registered for me at this moment. I updated my apartment lease to accommodate my new friend without hesitating, and likewise went to quickly purchase food, litter and toys and take them home before returning to the bookstore to pick up my newly adopted companion. The first thing the little creature did when I brought him home was to stand in front of my hallway mirror and practice his little black-cat Halloween dance, back arched, little paws scuttling back and forth. This was truly one of those events that was pure magic—unplanned, unexpected, even undreamed. But when it struck, I knew it was a comforting and enchanting sign from the Universe that I was on the right track. That letting go of some relationships and situations didn't mean that I was alone or isolated. It just meant that I was making space for connections and experiences that were more in alignment with my bruja ways.

Now, almost a year later, he is still the same shameless heart thief and writing companion, often sitting on the windowsill above my writing desk as I work. Smoke is my constant reminder that the world is full of magical things for those willing to slow down and move beyond surface living. Part of magical living is allowing for the possibility that things are not as they seem, or that magical possibilities are right around the corner. My familiar reminds me of both. He has helped me to embrace my inner Queen of Wands, the card in the tarot that is all about finding pleasure in the little things, stoking the fires of your inner joy, and finding empowerment in your individuality (she loves black cats and certainly doesn't care that many think them bad luck)—exactly what I write about and try to conjure in my daily life. My familiar has taught me to turn my face towards the sun, just like the sunflowers in that tarot card.

I'll give you another example. Years ago, I was preparing to teach a course on Gothic literature that looked at everything from 18th century British Gothic romances to modern Latinx urban legends like La Llorona, the Weeping Woman, who, story has it, threw her children into the river in a fit of rage after learning her husband cheated on her. The children drowned, and La Llorona now spends her afterlife trying to find her babies, often claiming young innocents as her own to suffer the same fate as her children hundreds of years ago. Spooky stuff! It was certainly scary enough to keep my younger self awake at night, thinking the howling wind was La Llorona crying for her children, and the tree branches scraping my window her hands trying to get inside and take me away. Naturally, her story spawned many a retelling (I've even written one myself in my first book, *Everyday Enchantments*), and I was eager to discuss with my students the archetype of this weeping woman.

I ordered an anthology of stories dedicated to her tragic tale. It was out of print, so I had to get it from a small bookseller online. The package arrived. Only the sellers didn't give me the right book. Instead, I got a copy of Sylvia Brinton Perera's *Descent to the Goddess: A Way of Initiation for Women*, a classic psychological text that was the exact same size and shape as the actual book I'd ordered. It was one of those autumn afternoons where it's still warm out, but the leaves are beginning to turn. I took the book out to my little patio with a cup of tea and read. I practiced some bookish synchronicity and opened the slim volume at random. The page outlined how a woman heals herself by turning inward and, like Persephone, going into the Underworld, or the unconscious, to explore her own mysteries.

The message was clear. I wasn't a weeping woman—indeed, I was allowed to let my grief go—and the way to do that was to move deeper into healing Goddess energy. You see, in slowing down and turning inward, I had also inadvertently created space for unexpected emotions to surface—things that got buried when I was moved too fast and got too busy. This book mix-up was a message to continue creating space to process and unpack things I needed to work through that I hadn't even known were there.

This included the ancestral trauma of Spanish patriarchy's violence against women, and the resulting bitterness those women passed down from generation to generation, recreating the trauma by stealing other people's children in the urban legend of La Llorona and, more symbolically, damaging a woman's fundamental innocence and inherent capacity to feel joy. It was the beginning of a long journey that brought to light much work that needed to be done to heal myself from the ancestral wounds of colonization and the institutionalized oppression of brown women in New Mexico, from wounds encoded in our DNA and hauntings passed on from generation to generation unless consciously worked through. Living beyond the expected for me inherently necessitated working through histories of oppression so that I could literally move—*live*—beyond those narratives.

Releasing myself from the hauntings of ancestral trauma became an essential part of creating a life less ordinary— and, sadly, coming to terms with the fact that all too often an ordinary life for the mestiza people was one of reinforced and internalized oppression. With magic, however, we are able to change the narrative. With magic, we are able to find hope and possibilities where once there was only heartbreak. With magic, we forge new paths.

Forging Your Own Path

One final note about living beyond the expected: It takes practice, just like any other form of magic. And one of the best ways to cultivate the playful trickster energy of the unexpected is to get serious about daydreaming, fantasizing, and wishing. We often think of those pursuits as frivolous, but they tell us a lot about the uncharted territories we want to explore. The secret desires and unconscious dreams. The barely-whispered hopes and the passions bubbling just under the surface. These are all energies that will nourish you as you make space for the unexpected, and learn that it is not something to be feared.

If that unbridled energy feels too unstructured—too scary— to indulge in right now, try this more structured, intentional exercise to help you tap into this form of Eros energy. Close your eyes and take a deep breath. Where does your mind go? Don't try to hold on to anything. Just observe. Notice how it makes you feel. Then gently release it. As you settle into your breath, gradually turn your thoughts to what makes you feel expansive. It could be a great story. A fabulous meal. A lover's kiss. Or a good night's rest. Whatever it is, allow those pleasant feelings to fill you up, from head to toe. Imagine that expansive energy pumping through your veins and tickling your skin. Don't hold it too tightly—rather, imagine it as abundant light within you and around you. Then think about why that abundant feeling resonated with you. Welcome that energy into your life and seek out stories, experiences, and small delights that fill you with the same openness.

Conclusion

Conjure Your Own Special Magic

Conjuring everyday magic is an ongoing process, one that changes with the seasons. Don't hesitate to let go of once-meaningful rituals in favor of new ones—the old ones have simply taught you all they need to. Our self-care needs also change as we age or become more sensitive to our minds, bodies, and spirits. Listen to that change.

It is my hope that this book has provided you with a working toolkit to explore your own, unique version of every magic, one that will become more and more distinctly yours as you practice it. Let it evolve. Let it flow. Trust your intuition and your increased sensitivity to your true nature. Celebrate your magical sanctuaries and your magical relationships. All that matters is that you keep intentionally conjuring. The more you practice, the stronger you'll get, the more easily the answers will come, because you'll have done the hard work to clear through blockages and listen to your instincts.

Conjuring everyday magic is an ongoing practice that takes time, patience, and the willingness to let go of preconceived notions of who you should be and what your life should look like. You have to get to know yourself. You have to open yourself to the possibility that you have divine wisdom. That your soul is a beautiful story, slowly revealing itself to you with each act of magic you feed it.

Questions to ask yourself:

What does my own unique magical signature look and feel like?
What are my routines as rituals that I use to replenish my magic?
What are my everyday conjurings that welcome magic into my life?

Take your time answering these final questions. Meditate on them. Let the answers unfold slowly and deliberately. They will develop over time, as you get more comfortable trusting your instincts and learning what your signature magic feels like.

In the end, magic is an act of trust. Of belief. In yourself. In your relationship to the world. In the cosmic Universe. In our profound ability to break the chains of ancestral hauntings and forge new stories. In the quiet truth that everyday life is filled with enchantments and mystic happenings if only we open ourselves to them. That's what makes this alternative kind of life so hard to cultivate, because when we believe in magic and our ability to conjure it, we then know that we are infinite. That we are the Divine Feminine. That we are pure bliss.

It's hard work, yes. But so worth it. Are you ready to go into the world to conjure your own special magic?

I know I am.

About the Author

Maria DeBlassie, Ph.D. is a native New Mexican mestiza blogger, award-winning writer, and award-winning educator living in the Land of Enchantment. Her first book, *Everyday Enchantments: Musings on Ordinary Magic & Daily Conjurings* (Moon Books 2018) and her ongoing blog, Enchantment Learning & Living, are about everyday magic, ordinary gothic, and the life of a kitchen witch. When she is not practicing her own brand of brujería, she's reading, teaching, and writing about witchy business, bodice rippers, and things that go bump in the night. She is forever looking for magic in her life and somehow always finding more than she thought was there. Find out more about Maria and conjuring everyday magic at www.mariadeblassie.com.

**MOON
BOOKS**

PAGANISM & SHAMANISM

What is Paganism? A religion, a spirituality, an alternative
belief system, nature worship? You can find support for all these
definitions (and many more) in dictionaries, encyclopaedias, and
text books of religion, but subscribe to any one and the truth will
evade you. Above all Paganism is a creative pursuit, an encounter
with reality, an exploration of meaning and an expression of the
soul. Druids, Heathens, Wiccans and others, all contribute their
insights and literary riches to the Pagan tradition. Moon Books
invites you to begin or to deepen your own encounter, right here,
right now.
If you have enjoyed this book, why not tell other readers by
posting a review on your preferred book site.

Recent bestsellers from Moon Books are:

Journey to the Dark Goddess
How to Return to Your Soul
Jane Meredith
Discover the powerful secrets of the Dark Goddess and
transform your depression, grief and pain into healing
and integration.
Paperback: 978-1-84694-677-6 ebook: 978-1-78099-223-5

Shamanic Reiki
Expanded Ways of Working with Universal Life Force Energy
Llyn Roberts, Robert Levy
Shamanism and Reiki are each powerful ways of healing; together,
their power multiplies. *Shamanic Reiki* introduces techniques to
help healers and Reiki practitioners tap ancient healing wisdom.
Paperback: 978-1-84694-037-8 ebook: 978-1-84694-650-9

Pagan Portals – The Awen Alone
Walking the Path of the Solitary Druid
Joanna van der Hoeven
An introductory guide for the solitary Druid, *The Awen Alone* will
accompany you as you explore, and seek out your own place
within the natural world.
Paperback: 978-1-78279-547-6 ebook: 978-1-78279-546-9

A Kitchen Witch's World of Magical Herbs & Plants
Rachel Patterson
A journey into the magical world of herbs and plants, filled with
magical uses, folklore, history and practical magic. By popular
writer, blogger and kitchen witch, Tansy Firedragon.
Paperback: 978-1-78279-621-3 ebook: 978-1-78279-620-6

Shaman Pathways – The Druid Shaman
Exploring the Celtic Otherworld
Danu Forest
A practical guide to Celtic shamanism with exercises and
techniques as well as traditional lore for exploring the Celtic
Otherworld.
Paperback: 978-1-78099-615-8 ebook: 978-1-78099-616-5

Traditional Witchcraft for the Woods and Forests
A Witch's Guide to the Woodland with Guided Meditations and
Pathworking
Mélusine Draco
A Witch's guide to walking alone in the woods, with guided
meditations and pathworking.
Paperback: 978-1-84694-803-9 ebook: 978-1-84694-804-6

Wild Earth, Wild Soul
A Manual for an Ecstatic Culture
Bill Pfeiffer
Imagine a nature-based culture so alive and so connected,
spreading like wildfire. This book is the first flame...
Paperback: 978-1-78099-187-0 ebook: 978-1-78099-188-7

Naming the Goddess
Trevor Greenfield
Naming the Goddess is written by over eighty adherents and
scholars of Goddess and Goddess Spirituality.
Paperback: 978-1-78279-476-9 ebook: 978-1-78279-475-2

Shapeshifting into Higher Consciousness
Heal and Transform Yourself and Our World with Ancient
Shamanic and Modern Methods
Llyn Roberts
Ancient and modern methods that you can use every day to
transform yourself and make a positive difference in the world.
Paperback: 978-1-84694-843-5 ebook: 978-1-84694-844-2

Readers of ebooks can buy or view any of these bestsellers by
clicking on the live link in the title. Most titles are published in
paperback and as an ebook. Paperbacks are available in traditional
bookshops. Both print and ebook formats are available online.

Find more titles and sign up to our readers' newsletter at
http://www.johnhuntpublishing.com/paganism
Follow us on Facebook at https://www.facebook.com/MoonBooks
and Twitter at https://twitter.com/MoonBooksJHP